MW00846343

ATI TEAS 6 Math Study Guide

TEAS Math Exam Preparation

with 5 Practice Tests

and Step-by-Step Solutions

ATI TEAS 6 Math Study Guide: TEAS Math Exam Preparation with 5 Practice Tests and Step-by-Step Solutions

ISBN-13: 978-1-949282-04-7

ISBN-10: 1-949282-04-X

For information on bulk discounts, please contact us at: email@examsam.com

How to Use This Publication

The first 150 problems in this book are organized into two sections: (1) Number Operations and Algebra and (2) Measurement and Data Analysis.

You should work through the concepts in practice questions 1 to 150 first. Pay special attention to the tips and hints after each question in the first section. The comments after each question tell you how to solve each type of problem that you will see on the real test and give you strategies for the day of your exam.

Each of the five practice tests at the end of the publication are like the actual exam, so they have 36 questions from all of the levels of difficulty. You should attempt the practice tests after you have studied all of the other material in the book. To simulate the real exam, you should allow 54 minutes to answer the 36 questions in each of the practice tests.

On the real test, you will not be penalized for guessing, so you should try to answer every question.

The answers and solutions for all of the practice test questions are provided at the end of the last practice exam.

Please note that for geometry questions, you should use 3.14 for π. Also note that the drawings in this publication are not to scale.

Formulas are provided after questions 1 to 150 as all of the concepts are introduced in these questions.

Should you wish to refer to the formulas later, please see the appendix to the book.

Free Basic Math Review

This study guide assumes some knowledge of basic math skills, such as addition, subtraction, multiplication, division, percentages, and decimals.

If you have difficulties with basic math problems or if you have been out of school for a while, you may wish to review our free basic math problems before taking the practice tests in this book.

The free review problems can be found at: www.examsam.com/math/numerical-skills/

TABLE OF CONTENTS

Measurement

Data Analysis & Statistics

ATI TEAS Practice Test Questions 81 to 150:

ATI TEAS Practice Tests 1 to 5:

Answers, Solutions, and Explanations:

ATI TEAS Practice Test Questions 1 to 80 with Study Tips and Formulas

Number Operations and Algebra

1) A company sells electronics online. The annual sales for the first three years of business were: $25,135, $32,787, and $47,004. What were the total sales for the past three years?
A) $101,326
B) $104,916
C) $104,926
D) $104,944

This is a question on adding whole numbers. The problem is asking for the total for all three years, so add the three figures together.

2) A customer gives the cashier $50 to pay for the items he purchased, which total $41.28. How much change should be given to the customer?
A) $7.82
B) $8.18
C) $8.27
D) $8.72

This is a question on subtracting whole numbers. To calculate the change, you need to take the amount of money the customer gives the cashier and subtract the amount of the purchase.

3) A car salesperson earns a $175 referral fee on every customer who accepts a customer service upgrade. The salesperson referred 8 customers for the service upgrade this month. How much did the salesperson earn in referral fees for the month?
A) $1050
B) $1200
C) $1225
D) $1400

This is a question on multiplying whole numbers. Multiplication problems will often include the words 'each' or 'every.' Multiply the amount of the referral fee by the number of customers to solve.

4) An employee's weekly pay is $535.50 and she works 30 hours per week. How much is she paid per hour?
A) $17.83
B) $17.84
C) $17.85
D) $18.34

This is a question on dividing whole numbers. Division problems will often include the word 'per.' Divide the total weekly amount by the number of hours to solve.

1

5)   Business losses are represented as negative numbers, while business profits are represented as positive numbers. A business makes the following profits and losses during a four week period: –$286, $953, $1502, and –$107. What was the total business profit or loss during these four weeks?
A) $2,026
B) $2,062
C) $2,080
D) –$2,026

This is a question on adding negative numbers. When you have to add a negative number to a positive number, you are subtracting. So, add the business profits and subtract the business losses to solve.

6)   Location below sea level is represented as a negative number. The location below sea level of Lake Alto is –35 meters. The location below sea level of Lake Bajo is 62 meters deeper than Lake Alto. What figure represents the location below sea level for Lake Bajo?
A) –97
B) 97
C) –62
D) –27

This is a question on subtracting negative numbers. The facts state that the location below sea level of Lake Bajo is 62 meters deeper than Lake Alto, so we need to subtract this figure from the location below sea level of Lake Alto. The location below sea level of Lake Alto is a negative number, so you are subtracting a negative from a negative.

7)   A company has completed 3/5 of a project. What figure below expresses the project completion amount as a decimal number?
A) 0.06
B) 0.60
C) 1.67
D) 3.00

This is a question on changing fractions to decimals. To express a fraction as a decimal, treat the line in the fraction as the division symbol and divide accordingly. Remember to be careful with the decimal placement in your final answer.

8)   A teacher reports attendance as a decimal figure, calculated as the number of students attending divided into the total number of students in the class. This week, the attendance was 0.55. What percentage best represents the attendance for this week?
A) 0.55%
B) 5.50%
C) 55.0%
D) 55.5%

This is a question on changing decimals to percentages. To express a decimal number as a percentage, move the decimal point two places to the right. Then add the percent sign.

9) An employee has used up 5/14 of his vacation days. Approximately what percentage of vacation days has the employee already used?
A) 0.357%
B) 2.800%
C) 3.571%
D) 35.7%

This is a question on changing fractions to decimals. Treat the line in the fraction as the division symbol and divide. Then move the decimal point two places to the right, and add the percent sign.

10) A driver has used 0.75 of the gas he last put in his car. What fraction best represents the amount of gas used?
A) 1/4
B) 2/5
C) 3/5
D) 3/4

This is a question on changing a decimal number to a fraction. You should be able to recognize the equivalent decimal numbers for commonly-used fractions such as ½ or ¾ for your exam. If you are unsure, perform division on the answer choices to solve.

11) It is reported that 33% of all new stores close within five years of opening. What fraction best represents this percentage?
A) 1/3
B) 1/4
C) 1/5
D) 2/3

This is a question on changing a percentage to a fraction. You should be able to recognize the equivalent fractions for commonly-used percentages for the test. If you are unsure of the answer, perform division on the answer choices to solve.

12) A carpet store is offering 45% off in a sale this month. What decimal number below best represents the percentage off?
A) 0.0045
B) 0.0450
C) 0.4500
D) 4.5000

This is a question on changing percentages to decimals. Any given percentage is out of 100%, so we divide by 100 to express a percentage as a decimal. So, move the decimal point two places to the left and remove the percent sign.

13) A bakery has to pay 36 cents for each pound of flour it buys. It decides to buy $14^{1}/_{4}$ pounds of flour today. How much will it have to pay?
A) $3.60
B) $5.13
C) $5.31
D) $142.50

3

14) A bookkeeper has just been with a client for 0.35 hours. Approximately how many minutes did the bookkeeper spend with this client?
A) 3.5 minutes
B) 5.8 minutes
C) 21 minutes
D) 35 minutes

15) A flower store charges $24 for a small arrangement of flowers. A customer will get a $5 discount if he or she provides his or her own vase for the small arrangement. This month, there were 12 customers who ordered small arrangements and provided their own vases. How much money in total did the flower store make on arrangements sold to these 12 customers?
A) $228
B) $282
C) $288
D) $348

16) A bricklayer works for a construction company. He laid bricks for 7 hours per day for 4 days on one job. The customer was billed $45 per hour for his work, and he was paid $25 per hour. After the bricklayer's wages have been paid, how much money did the company make for his work on this job?
A) $175
B) $180
C) $315
D) $560

17) A pharmacist owns a local drug store. Last week, she filled 250 prescriptions in 40 hours. Assuming that each prescription takes the same amount of time, how many minutes should it take her to fill a single prescription?
A) 9.6 minutes
B) 6.25 minutes
C) 3.75 minutes
D) 0.16 minutes

18) A truck driver delivered 120 orders this week. She delivered 105 of the orders on time. What percentage of the driver's orders was delivered on time?
A) 0.875%
B) 8.75%
C) 87.5%
D) 0.125%

This is a question with two operations. Take the amount of orders that were delivered on time and divide by the amount of total orders. Then convert to a percentage.

19) A scientist measures cell growth or attrition. Each day a measurement is taken. Cell growth is represented as a positive figure, while cell attrition is represented as a negative figure. On Monday cell growth was 27, and for all days Tuesday through Friday, cell attrition was 13 per day. What number represents total cell growth or attrition for these five days?
A) 25
B) −25
C) 40
D) −40

This is a question on multiplying negative numbers. Cell attrition is a negative number, so perform multiplication to get the total for Tuesday through Friday. Then add the cell growth for Monday to solve.

20) A vegetable farmer works until noon each day. The chart below shows the amounts of cucumbers per hour that she picked one morning:
7:00 to 8:00   23 cucumbers
8:00 to 9:00   25 cucumbers
9:00 to 10:00   26 cucumbers
10:00 to 11:00   24 cucumbers
11:00 to 12:00   22 cucumbers
On average, how many cucumbers did the farmer pick per hour?
A) 23
B) 24
C) 25
D) 26

This is a question on calculating averages. To find the average, you need to add all of the amounts to get the total, and then divide the total by the number of hours.

21) A local company makes one particular kind of concrete. For this concrete, 2 units of sand have to be added to every 3 units of cement powder used. A batch of this concrete that has 66 units of cement powder is being made. How many units of sand should be added to this batch?
A) 2
B) 3
C) 22
D) 44

This is a question on a simple ratio. Take the 66 units of cement powder for the current batch and divide by the 3 units stated in the original ratio. Then multiply this result by the 2 units of sand stated in the original ratio to solve.

22) It is company policy that the ratio of employees to supervisors should be 50:1. So, for every 50 employees in a company, there should be 1 supervisor. If there are 255 employees, how many supervisors are there?

A) 1
B) 2
C) 3
D) 5

This is another question on a simple ratio. The problem states that we are working with a ratio, so the employees and the supervisors form separate groups. First, add the two groups together. Then take the total amount of employees stated in the problem and divide this by the figure you have just calculated to get the amount of supervisors.

23) A report shows that 2 out of every 20 employees in a particular company are interested in applying for a promotion. If the company has 480 employees in total, how many employees are interested in applying for a promotion?

A) 20
B) 24
C) 42
D) 48

This is a question on a simple proportion. Problems on proportions often use the phrase 'out of.' The problem uses the phrase '2 out of every 20 employees' so we know that there are 2 employees who form a subset within each group of 20. So, take the total number of employees and divide this by 20. Then multiply this result by the amount in the subset to solve.

24) A mechanic spent from 8:10 to 8:22 changing three wheel covers on a car. At this rate, how many wheel covers could he change per hour?

A) 3
B) 5
C) 15
D) 20

This is a question on calculating a simple rate. Calculate the amount of time in minutes that was spent on the three wheel covers. Then calculate the time in minutes needed to change 1 wheel cover. Then divide this amount into 60 minutes to solve.

25) A fencing company put up $15^2/_8$ yards of fence for one customer and $13^5/_8$ yards of fence for another customer. How many yards of fence did the company put up for both customers in total?

A) $28^3/_8$
B) $28^5/_8$
C) $28^7/_8$
D) $28^7/_{16}$

This is a question on adding fractions that have a common denominator. First, add the whole numbers that are in front of each fraction. Then add the fractions. If you have two fractions that have the same denominator, which is the number on the bottom of the fraction, you add the numerators and keep the common denominator. Then combine the new whole number and the new fraction to solve.

26) A food company fills gourmet food boxes with various products. So far today, $2\frac{3}{8}$ boxes have been filled for one order and $4\frac{1}{8}$ boxes have been filled for another order. How many total boxes have been filled so far today?

A) $6\frac{1}{2}$

B) $6\frac{1}{4}$

C) $6\frac{3}{4}$

D) $6\frac{3}{16}$

This is another question on adding fractions that have a common denominator. Follow the same steps as for the previous question, but also simplify the fraction to solve. This means that you have to reduce the numerator and denominator by dividing them by the same number, which is known as a common factor.

27) A customer has just placed an order to have an awning made for his front window. According to the measurements, $5\frac{3}{16}$ yards of canvas will be needed to make the awning. However, the customer calls later to say that his initial measurement was incorrect, and only $4\frac{1}{16}$ yards of canvas is actually needed to make the awning. Which fraction below represents the amount by which the amount of canvas has been reduced?

A) $1\frac{1}{8}$

B) $1\frac{1}{16}$

C) $1\frac{1}{32}$

D) $1\frac{3}{16}$

This is a question on subtracting fractions with a common denominator. First, subtract the whole numbers, and then subtract the fractions. If you have two fractions that have the same denominator, you subtract the numerators and keep the common denominator. Then simplify the fraction. Finally, combine the whole number and the simplified fraction to solve.

28) Certain additives need to be placed in a bottle to make a particular product. The company measures each additive in decimal units, with 1 unit representing the filled bottle. The bottle contains 0.25 units of additive A, 0.50 units of additive B, and 0.10 units of additive C. Which of the following represents, in terms of units, how full the bottle currently is?

A) 08.5

B) 0.85

C) 0.90

D) 0.95

This is a question on adding commonly-known decimals. Add the three figures together to solve. Remember to be sure to put the decimal point in the correct place when you work out the solution.

29) A recent survey shows that 50% of your customers rated your service as excellent and 25% rated your service as very good. What percentage below represents the total amount of customers who rated your service either excellent or very good?

A) 25%

B) 50%

C) 75%

D) 85%

This is a question on adding commonly-known percentages. Simply add the percentages together to solve.

7

30) A customer has just ordered 5 units of a product. Each unit of the product takes $1\frac{1}{4}$ hours to make. How much time is needed to make this order?
   A) 5 hours and 25 minutes
   B) 5 hours and 55 minutes
   C) 6 hours and 4 minutes
   D) 6 hours and 15 minutes

This is a question on multiplying a mixed number by a whole number of units. First, multiply the whole numbers. Then multiply the whole number of units by the fraction. Then convert this improper fraction to a mixed number. Add the whole number and the mixed number, and convert to hours and minutes to solve.

31) A dressmaker who works in a tailoring shop is trying to decide what setting to use on the sewing machine. She has tried the 1/8 inch stitch but has realized that it is too small. The stitches on the machine are sized in 1/32 increments. What size stitch should she try next?
   A) 3/16
   B) 5/32
   C) 6/16
   D) 6/32

This is a question on performing calculations on fractions with different denominators. Convert 1/8 to the following equivalent fraction: 1/8 = ?/32

32) Amal runs a souvenir store that sells key rings. She can get 50 key rings from her first supplier for 50 cents each. She can get the same 50 keys rings from her second supplier for $30 in total or from her third supplier for $27.50. How much will she pay if she gets the best deal?
   A) $25.00
   B) $25.25
   C) $25.50
   D) $27.50

This is a question on finding the best deal when you have to perform a one-step calculation. Read the facts carefully, work out the total prices for all three suppliers, and then compare prices.

33) A budget hotel charges $45 per night or $280 per week. If a guest stays at the hotel for 9 nights, what is the least that he will pay for his stay?
   A) $280
   B) $315
   C) $325
   D) $370

This is a question on finding the best deal when you have to perform two-step calculations. Determine the duration of the stay in weeks and nights. Then add the cost for 1 week to the cost for 2 days to solve.

34) The price of an item is normally $15, but customers with a loyalty card can purchase it at the discounted price of $12. What percentage best represents the discount awarded to these customers?
   A) 3%
   B) 5%
   C) 15%
   D) 20%

This is a question on calculating the percentage of a discount. Divide the dollar amount of the discount by the original price to get the percentage of the discount.

35) A retail ceramics store sells mugs and bowls. It buys one type of mug for $3 and sells it for $9. It uses the same percentage mark up on one type of bowl that it buys for $4. What figure below represents the sales price of the bowl?
A) $6
B) $8
C) $12
D) $16

This is a question on calculating a markup. You need to calculate the percentage for the markup on the first product and apply this percentage markup to the second product. Remember to use the percentage markup, rather than a dollar value. You may need the following formulas if you don't already know how to calculate markup: Dollar value of markup = Sales price in dollars − Cost in dollars; Percentage markup = Dollar value of markup ÷ Cost in dollars

36) A company got $20 off of an order. This amounted to a 25% discount off the order. What would the company have paid without the discount?
A) $4
B) $5
C) $25
D) $80

This is a question on calculating a reverse percentage. To calculate a reverse percentage you need to divide, rather than multiply. So, take the dollar value of the discount and divide by the percentage to solve.

37) What is the largest possible product of two even integers whose sum is 22?
A) 11
B) 44
C) 100
D) 120

You will see mathematical communication problems that ask you to translate sentences into equations or computations. Since the solution is asking for the product of two integers, you should divide 22 by 2 for your first step.

38) Maria sells soft drinks in a convenience store that she runs. She can buy 240 soft drinks from one supplier for 25 cents each or from a different supplier for $58 for all 240 drinks. Both suppliers are in the same state, so she has to pay a sales tax of 6.5% on either purchase. If she chooses the best price for the soft drinks, including tax, how much will she pay in total?
A) $58.00
B) $60.00
C) $61.77
D) $63.90

39) A picture framing store can make 20 small frames in 4 days or 21 large frames in 3 days. A customer has just placed an order with for 40 small frames and 64 large ones. Approximately how many days will it take to make them all?
   A) 7
   B) 11
   C) 14
   D) 17

This is a question on calculating production rates by unit. Determine the unit rates per day for each of the products by dividing the output by the number of days. Then divide the rates into the amount of items ordered to solve.

40) The report on a production order shows that 12.5% of the work has been completed in the past 4 days. If work continues at the same rate, how many more days will be required in order to finish the order?
   A) 3
   B) 4
   C) 28
   D) 32

This is a question on calculating rate by time. Calculate the percentage of work completed per day, and then determine how many days are needed for the job.

41) When 1523.48 is divided by 100, which digit of the resulting number is in the tenths place?
   A) 1
   B) 2
   C) 3
   D) 4

This question assesses your understanding of decimals. Remember that the number after the decimal is in the tenths place, the second number after the decimal is in the hundredths place, and the third number after the decimal is in the thousandths place.

42) The volume of item A is 15 units less than 5 times the volume of item B.
   Which of the following equations best expresses the above statement?
   A) $A - 15 \times 5 = B$
   B) $(A - 15) \times 5 = B$
   C) $A = 5B - 15$
   D) $A = 15 - 5B$

You will have to make equations from narrative information on the exam, like in this question. It is usually best to begin your solution with the last thing mentioned in the question, so make an expression for 5 times B for your first step.

Algebraic Expressions

43) Evaluate: $2x^2 - x + 5$ if $x = -2$
    A) 2
    B) 7
    C) 15
    D) 17

Step 1 – To perform the operations on the first term of the equation, multiply –2 by itself to square it. Then multiply this result by 2. Step 2 – To get your final answer, take the result from step 1 and subtract –2 and add 5.

44) Solve for x: $-6x + 5 = -19$
    A) 2
    B) 4
    C) 6
    D) 8

Isolate x to one side of the equation by subtracting 5 from both sides of the equation. Then multiply each side of the new equation by –6 to isolate x and solve.

45) If $4x - 3(x + 2) = -3$, then $x = $?
    A) 9
    B) 3
    C) 1
    D) –3

Multiply the terms inside the parentheses by the –3 in front of the set of parentheses. Then simplify and isolate x to one side of the equation to solve.

46) If $\frac{3}{4}x - 2 = 4$, $x = $?
    A) $\frac{8}{3}$

    B) $\frac{1}{8}$

    C) 8

    D) –8

Multiply each side of the equation by $\frac{4}{3}$ to get rid of the fraction. Then simplify the remaining new improper fraction and add the result of the simplified fraction to both sides of the equation solve.

47) What is the value of $\frac{x-3}{2-x}$ when $x = 1$?
    A) 2
    B) –2
    C) $^1/_2$
    D) $-^1/_2$

Substitute 1 for the value of x. Then perform the subtraction in the numerator and the subtraction in the dominator. Then simplify the resulting fraction to solve.

Linear Inequalities

48) $50 - \dfrac{3x}{5} \geq 41$, then $x \leq$?
    A) 15
    B) 25
    C) 41
    D) 50

> Step 1: Isolate the whole numbers to one side of the inequality. Step 2: Get rid of the fraction by multiplying each side by 5. Step 3: Divide to simplify further. Step 4: Isolate the variable to solve.

Absolute Value Equations and Inequalities

49)   Find the equivalent: $| 14 - 82 |$
    A) −68
    B) 68
    C) −96
    D) 96

50)   Find the value of x that satisfies the following inequality: $|- 47 + 35| + x \geq 0$
    A) $x \leq -12$
    B) $x \geq -12$
    C) $x \leq 12$
    D) $x \geq 12$

> When you see numbers inside two lines like this, you are being asked for the absolute value. Absolute value is always a positive number. For example: $| -7| = 7$

Measurement

51) A land surveyor must measure the distance between landmarks. She has measured a distance between two landmarks and discovered that it is 538 feet. What is the approximate distance between the landmarks in terms of meters?
   A) 45
   B) 164
   C) 1367
   D) 1765

This is a question on using a formula with a measurement. Use the following formula and multiply to solve: 1 foot = 0.3048 meters

52) A physical therapist measures how far her clients are able to walk during each session. One client walked 123 feet and 6 inches during his first session and 138 feet and 8 inches during his second session. What is the combined total of the distance walked for the two sessions?
   A) 261 feet 24 inches
   B) 261 feet 6 inches
   C) 262 feet 8 inches
   D) 262 feet 2 inches

This is a question on performing a calculation with mixed units. It is usually easiest to perform one calculation with the feet and another with the inches. You may need to convert the total inches back to feet and inches if there are more than 12 inches in the second calculation.

53) A nutritionist advises clients and sells supplements to them. A box containing the supplements weighs 8 pounds and 5 ounces when full. The box itself weighs 7 ounces when it is empty. Each supplement weighs 0.75 ounces. About how many supplements should be in the box?
   A) 168
   B) 177
   C) 178
   D) 186

This is a question on performing conversions within systems of measurement. Here we have to convert between pounds and ounces. Convert the total weight of the product (excluding the box weight) to ounces then divide the total ounces by the ounces per unit to solve. 1 pound = 16 ounces

54) A garden store fertilizes and treats customers' lawns. One customer wants to fertilize and treat his lawn, which is $50^1/_4$ feet by $60^1/_4$ feet in size. The cost of the fertilizer and treatment is $5.25 per square yard. To the nearest dollar, how much will it cost the customer to fertilize and treat his lawn?
   A) $177
   B) $1,766
   C) $5,298
   D) $15,895

This is a question on working with quantities that contain fractions. Convert the mixed numbers to decimals and multiply. Then convert to square yards and solve. 1 square yard = 9 square feet

55) It is company policy to have at least 60 yards of dark black yarn in stock at the start of every month. Inventory has been taken this morning and there are 2 balls of dark black yarn that are 75 inches each and 4 balls of dark black yarn that are 25¹/₄ inches each in stock. This yarn must be purchased in 5-yard-long balls. How many balls of yarn should be purchased in order to replenish the stock?

A) 10
B) 11
C) 33
D) 36

This is a question on working with fractional units. Calculate the amount of remaining stock in inches, and then convert from inches to yards. Then calculate the amount required to restock. Remember that it is not possible to buy a fractional part of a ball, so you have to round up to solve.

56) A company that manufactures liquid cosmetics needs to test a 0.75 gram sample of an active ingredient of a liquid cosmetic. The correct concentration ratio is 50 milligrams of active ingredient to 1.5 milliliters of liquid. How many milliliters of liquid should be added to the sample?

A) 0.000015
B) 0.000225
C) 15.0
D) 22.5

This is a question on converting grams to milligrams. Convert to grams (1 gram = 1,000 milligrams). Then apply the correct ratio to solve.

57) A carpenter creates triangular-shaped corner shelves from oak and other wood for sale to furniture and home stores. He needs to report the area of each shelf to the buyer as part of the sales agreement. He needs to calculate the area of a triangular-shaped shelf that has a base of 12 inches and a height of 14 inches. What is the area of this shelf in square inches?

A) 56
B) 84
C) 168
D) 1728

Use the formula for the area of a triangle: ½ (base × height)

58) Triangle ABC is a right-angled triangle. Side A and side B form the right angle, and side C is the hypotenuse. If A = 3 and B = 2, what is the length of side C?

A) 5
B) $\sqrt{5}$
C) $\sqrt{13}$
D) 13

The hypotenuse is the side of the triangle that is opposite the right angle. To calculate the length of the hypotenuse in right triangles, you will need the Pythagorean Theorem. According to the theorem, the length of the hypotenuse (represented by side C) is equal to the square root of the sum of the squares of the other two sides of the triangle (represented by A and B). For any right triangle with sides A, B, and C, you need to remember this formula:

$$\text{hypotenuse length C} = \sqrt{A^2 + B^2}$$

59) A carpenter is making a special triangular-shaped corner shelf for a custom order. The customer lives in a 300-year-old house, so the walls are not completely straight and the corners are not completely square. He needs to make a triangular shelf that will have one 44° angle and one 47° angle. What is the measurement in degrees of the third angle of this shelf?
A) 45°
B) 45.5°
C) 89°
D) 90°

The sum of all three angles in any triangle is always equal to 180 degrees.

60) A real-estate developer has recently purchased a circular-shaped tower. The first floor of the building has been divided into 5 pie-shaped segments that join at the center of the circle. The first segment measures 82° along the outside edge. The second segment has a measurement of 79°, the third has a measurement of 46° and the fourth has a measurement = 85°. What is the measurement in degrees of outside edge the fifth segment?
A) 48
B) 49
C) 58
D) 68

A complete circle measures 360 degrees.

61) A building project has a circular tower. The floor of the tower, which has a 12-foot radius, needs to be filled in with concrete. In order to do this, the area of the floor of the tower needs to be calculated. What is the approximate area of the floor of the tower in square feet?
A) 452.16
B) 376.80
C) 226.08
D) 37.68

This is a question on calculating the area of a circle. The formula for the area of a circle is as follows: circle area ≈ 3.14 × (radius)^2

62) A technician measures the wear on tractor tires. In order to determine the rate of wear, the circumference of each tire must be determined first. The tire currently being measured has a diameter of 46.5 inches. What is the circumference?
A) 23.500 inches
B) 73.005 inches
C) 146.01 inches
D) 292.02 inches

This is a question on calculating the circumference of a circle. Circumference ≈ 3.14 × diameter

63) Becky is making a patchwork quilt that is going to be 6 feet long and 5 feet wide. What will the surface area of the quilt be in square feet?
A) 11
B) 22
C) 25
D) 30

This is a question on calculating the area of a rectangle. Area of a rectangle = length × width

15

64) A fence needs to be put around a field that is 12 yards long and 9 yards wide. What figure below best represents the perimeter of this field in yards?
   A) 21
   B) 42
   C) 54
   D) 72

This is a question on calculating the perimeter of a rectangle. Remember not to confuse area and perimeter as they are different calculations. Perimeter of a rectangle = 2 × (length + width)

65) A circular fish pond is being designing for your local park. The pond has an area of about 78.5 square feet. What is the approximate diameter of the pond?
   A) 5 feet
   B) 10 feet
   C) 15.7 feet
   D) 25 feet

You need to use the formula in reverse for this question, so use 3.14 for π and divide by 3.14, instead of multiplying by 3.14. Remember that diameter is double the radius, so if the radius is 3 feet, for example, the diameter is 6 feet. Remember that the formula is: circle area ≈ 3.14 × (radius)^2.

66) A tank that holds dye is 5 feet wide, 8 feet long, and 3 feet high. How many cubic feet of dye can the tank hold when it is completely full?
   A) 15
   B) 24
   C) 40
   D) 120

The length, width, and height are different measurements, so we need the formula for the volume of a rectangular solid or box: volume = *length × width × height*

67) A cube footrest has a side length of 18 inches. How many cubic inches of filling should be placed inside the footrest?
   A) 5,832
   B) 729
   C) 324
   D) 72

For this problem, we need to calculate the volume of a cube. The formula for the volume of a cube is as follows: cube volume = (*length of side*)^3

68) A company processes dairy products. Milk is stored in a spherical storage tank that is 72 inches across on the inside. The tank is now 80% full of milk. What is the volume of the milk in the tank?
   A) 156,267
   B) 156,627
   C) 159,333
   D) 195,333

This is a question on calculating spherical volume. You need the following formula: Volume of a sphere ≈ 4/3 × 3.14 × radius^3. Use the formula and multiply by the percentage stated in the problem.

69) A cylindrical tank has a 5 meter radius and is 21 meters in height. What is the volume of the tank?
   A) 329.70
   B) 1648.5
   C) 549.50
   D) 659.40

This is a question on calculating cylindrical volume. Cylinder volume $\approx$ 3.14 × radius^2 × height. Substitute the values into the formula, and perform the operations in the formula to solve.

70) A confection company manufactures three different sizes of ice cream cones. The large cones are 6 inches high and have a 1.5 inch radius, the medium cones are 5 inches high and have a 1 inch radius, and the small cones are 4 inches high and have a 0.5 inch radius. What is the difference between the volume in cubic inches of the large cone and the medium cone?
   A) 4.19
   B) 5.23
   C) 8.90
   D) 14.13

This is a question on calculating differences in volumes. Cone volume $\approx$ (3.14 × radius^2 × height) ÷ 3. Calculate the difference between the volumes of the two cones to solve.

Data Analysis

For questions 71 to 76, study the charts carefully, paying attention to the legends and labels on each one. Be sure to read each question carefully to be sure what calculation or conclusion you need to make.

Look at the bar chart below and answer questions 71 to 74.

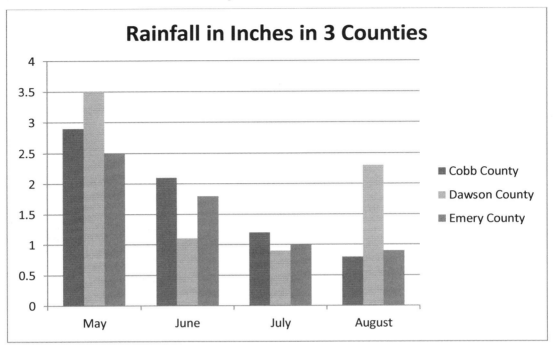

71) Which of the following statements is supported by the data above?
   A) Cobb County suffered a drought in the month of August.
   B) The amount of rainfall for Dawson County was relatively unchanged from month to month.
   C) The amount of rainfall for Cobb County decreased every month for the four months represented on the chart.
   D) The amount of rainfall for each county for September can be accurately predicted using the information above.

72) What was the approximate difference in the amount of rainfall for Dawson County and Emery County for June?
   A) Dawson County had 0.6 more inches of rainfall than Emery County.
   B) Emery County had 0.6 more inches of rainfall than Dawson County.
   C) Dawson County had 1.1 fewer inches of rainfall than Emery County.
   D) Emery County had 1.1 fewer inches of rainfall than Dawson County.

73) What was the approximate total rainfall for Emery County for all four months?
   A) 6.2 inches
   B) 6.8 inches
   C) 7.0 inches
   D) 7.4 inches

74) Which figure below best represents the total amount of rainfall in inches for the county had the least amount of rainfall for all four months in total?
   A) 6.2
   B) 6.9
   C) 7
   D) 7.8

Look at the pie chart and information below and answer questions 75 and 76.

A zoo has reptiles, birds, quadrupeds, and fish. At the end of last year, they had a total of 1,500 creatures living in the zoo. The pie chart below shows percentages by category for the 1,500 creatures at the end of last year. At the end of this year, the zoo still has 1,500 creatures, but reptiles constitute 40%, quadrupeds 21%, and fish 16%. The percentage of the creatures that the zoo has from year-to-year is based on the results of an end-of-year customer preference questionnaire.

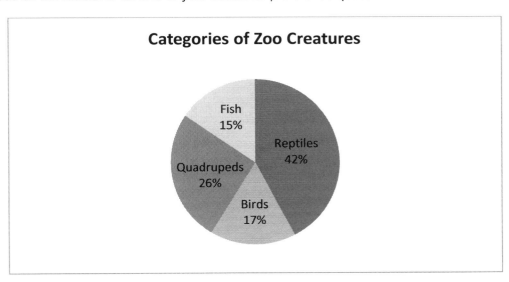

75) How many reptiles are in the zoo at the start of the year?
   A) 225
   B) 255
   C) 390
   D) 630

76) Which one of the following statements is supported by the data?
   A) There were 165 more fish than quadrupeds at the start of the year.
   B) The customers who responded to the questionnaire at the end of this year had a higher preference for fish than those of the previous year.
   C) There were 90 fewer birds at the end of the year than at the beginning of the year.
   D) The zookeepers prefer the reptiles over the other zoo creatures.

Statistics:

Look at the table below and answer questions 77 to 80.

Sunday	Monday	Tuesday	Wednesday	Thursday	Friday	Saturday
−10°F	−9°F	1°F	6°F	8°F	13°F	12°F

77) What was the median temperature for the week?
    A) 1°
    B) 3°
    C) 6°
    D) 22°

78) What was the mean temperature for the week?
    A) 1°
    B) 3°
    C) 6°
    D) 22°

79) What was the mode in the temperatures for the week?
    A) 1°
    B) 3°
    C) 8°
    D) no mode

80) What is the range in the temperatures for the week?
    A) −2°
    B) −3°
    C) −23°
    D) 23°

Mean: The mean is the same thing as the arithmetic average. In order to calculate the mean, you simply add up the values of all of the items in the set, and then divide by the number of items in the set.

Mode: Mode is the value that occurs most frequently in a data set. For example, if 10 students scored 85 on a test, 6 students scored 90, and 4 students scored 80, the mode score is 85.

Median: The median is the number that is in the middle of the set when the numbers are in ascending order.

Range: To calculate range, the lowest value in the data set is deducted from the highest value in the data set.

ATI TEAS Practice Test Questions 81 to 150

Number Operations and Algebra

81) The depth of a well is represented as a negative number. The first well that was dug this week measured –92 meters, and the second well dug this week was 120 meters deeper than the first well. What figure below represents the depth of the second well?
A) –120
B) 120
C) 212
D) –212

82) Matthew sells kitchen cupboards for a chain store. He gets a $350 commission for every set of kitchen cupboards he sells. This week, he sold 11 sets of kitchen cupboards. What is his commission for the week?
A) $350
B) $361
C) $3500
D) $3850

83) A company sells artwork and prints online. The sales for the first four months of business were: $2516, $3482, $4871, and $5267. What were the total sales for the first four months?
A) $16,082
B) $16,136
C) $16,145
D) $16,181

84) A health club received $2,496 this month for monthly membership fees. If each member pays the same amount in monthly fees and there are 52 members, what is the monthly membership fee?
A) $4
B) $8
C) $48
D) $52

85) A customer gives a cashier $150 to pay for the items she purchased, which total $127.82. How much change should the cashier give the customer?
A) $22.18
B) $22.27
C) $22.28
D) $22.72

86) Investment losses are represented as negative numbers, while investment profits are represented as positive numbers. An investor makes the following profits and losses during a six month period: –$1205, $532, $875, –$1359, $1436, and –$982. What was the total investment profit or loss during these six months?
A) –$703
B) $703
C) $1707
D) $2015

87) You have already sold $^6/_{25}$ of your inventory this month. Approximately what percentage of your inventory have you already sold?
A) 0.24%
B) 24%
C) 2.40%
D) 4.167%

88) 80% of a store's sales are from sunglasses and other accessories. What fraction best represents this percentage?
A) $^3/_4$
B) $^3/_5$
C) $^4/_5$
D) $^4/_6$

89) A business reports profit margin, calculated as net income in relation to sales revenue, as a decimal figure. Last year, the profit margin was 0.32. What percentage best represents the profit margin for last year?
A) 0.32%
B) 3.20%
C) 32.0%
D) 32.2%

90) An eyeglasses store is offering 25% off in a sale this month. What decimal number below best represents the percentage off?
A) 0.0025
B) 0.2500
C) 2.5000
D) 25.000

91) An employee has to package 50 identical items in individual packages. She has completed 0.24 of the entire job. How many items has she packaged so far?
A) 6 items
B) 12 items
C) 18 items
D) 24 items

92) A business enterprise has already 0.20 of its monthly budget at the end of the second week of the month. What fraction best represents the amount of the budget that has been spent?
A) 1/8
B) 1/4
C) 1/5
D) 6/8

93) A convenience store sells candy by the ounce. Customers have to pay 20 cents for each ounce of candy they buy. One customer buys $15^1/_2$ ounces of candy. How much will he have to pay for this purchase?
A) $2.10
B) $3.00
C) $3.10
D) $22.50

94) Last week, 210 order forms were completed in 35 hours. Assuming that each order form takes the same amount of time to complete, how many minutes should it take to complete an individual order form?
A) 0.10 minutes
B) 1.0 minutes
C) 10 minutes
D) 0.6 minutes

95) A census has revealed that 7 out of every 10 families in a certain city have school-age children living at home. If there are 4,500 families living in this city, how many families with school-age children living at home are in the city?
A) 643
B) 700
C) 1,350
D) 3,150

96) A business analsist calculates the cash flow needs of businesses. Positive cash flow is represented as a positive figure, while negative cash flow is represented as a negative figure. Cash flow figures for a particular business were as follows: Week 1 –$1,503; Week 2 $2,476; Week 3 –$3,087; Week 4 $986. What was the total cash flow for these four weeks?
A) −1128
B) 1128
C) −1848
D) −1155

97) A novelty store charges $12 for a certain gift. A customer will need to pay $1.50 more per gift if he or she wants to have it gift wrapped. This month, 51 customers purchased this gift and requested gift wrap. How much money in total did the store make on gifts sold to these 51 customers?
A) $668.50
B) $688.50
C) $612.00
D) $621.00

98) A company makes stained glass panels for windows. One employee worked 7 hours on a job each day for 6 days for one customer. The customer was billed $30 per hour for the employee's work, and the employee was paid $18 per hour. How much money did the company make on these windows after paying the employee's wages?
A) $108
B) $126
C) $504
D) $756

99) A company received 132 satisfactory responses from customers on a customer satisfaction questionnaire. 150 customers were questioned for this particular questionnaire. What percentage of the customers' responses was satisfactory?
A) 0.88%
B) 8.80%
C) 82.0%
D) 88.0%

100) A factory line worker assembles the following number of units over a five-day period. Day 1: 106 units; Day 2: 110 units; Day 3: 108 units; Day 4: 112 units; Day 5: 104 units. On average, how many units did the worker complete per day?
A) 108
B) 115
C) 135
D) 180

101) An independent consultant undertakes projects for clients. The completion status of the project is reported at the end of the week in terms of whole units plus fractional units. This week, $5^5/_8$ projects have been completed for one client and $3^3/_8$ projects have been completed for another client. What is the total completion status for these two projects at the end of this week?
A) $2^1/_4$
B) 8
C) $8^7/_8$
D) 9

102) A store creates custom-made curtains and draperies by special order for customers. A customer placed an order, which according to the initial measurements, required $9^5/_{12}$ yards of fabric. However, the measurements were taken again later and it was determined that the initial measurement was incorrect. In fact, $10^7/_{12}$ yards of fabric is actually needed for this order. Which amount below represents the change to this order?
A) $1^1/_6$ more yards needed
B) $1^1/_6$ fewer yards needed
C) $1^1/_3$ more yards needed
D) $1^1/_3$ fewer yards needed

103) A company manufactures sails for sailboats. $25^7/_{16}$ yards of sailcloth is needed for one order and $32^2/_{16}$ yards of sailcloth is needed for another order. How many yards of sailcloth are needed for both of these orders in total?
A) $57^1/_4$
B) $57^3/_{16}$
C) $57^9/_{16}$
D) $57^3/_4$

104) A gardener has to mix herbicide as part of her job. The herbicide comes as a liquid that needs to be diluted with water. According to the instructions, 5 ounces of water has to be added to every 2 ounces of herbicide liquid that is used. A mixture of the herbicide is being made now, and it should contain 84 ounces of herbicide liquid. How many ounces of water should be added to this mixture?
A) 420
B) 210
C) 84.0
D) 42.0

105) The human resources department mandates that the ratio of upper-level managers to mid-level managers should be 2:3. So, for every 2 upper-level managers in the company, there should be 3 mid-level managers. If there are 87 mid-level managers, how many upper-level managers are there?
A) 58
B) 44
C) 36
D) 13

106) Sarah worked from 9:15 to 9:35 creating 2 hand-made birthday cards. At this rate, how many birthday cards will she make during an 8-hour day?
A) 6
B) 12
C) 36
D) 48

107) A company mixes chemicals in a tank to make a sealing treatment for driveways. The company measures each additive in decimal units, with 100 units representing the filled tank. The tank contains 75.25 units of Chemical X, 10.75 units of Chemical Y, and 3.20 units of Chemical Z. Which of the following represents, in terms of units, how full the tank currently is?
A) 99.2
B) 89.2
C) 88.3
D) 80.2

108) A company's online survey results show that 45% of its online reviews are 5-star and 35% of its online reviews are 4-star. What percentage below represents the total amount of online 5-star and 4-star reviews?
A) 80%
B) 70%
C) 45%
D) 35%

109) A home decorating business has just received an order for 5 tea-light candle holders. Each tea-light candle holder takes $2\frac{1}{2}$ hours to make. How much time is needed to make all five holders?
A) 10 hours and 25 minutes
B) 10 hours and 30 minutes
C) 10 hours and 50 minutes
D) 12 hours and 30 minutes

110) Jason does the high jump for his high school track and field team. His first jump is at 3.246 meters. His second is 3.331 meters, and his third is 3.328 meters. If the height of each jump is rounded to the nearest one-hundredth of a meter (also called a centimeter), what is the estimate of the total height for all three jumps combined?
A) 9.80
B) 9.89
C) 9.90
D) 9.91

111) A road maintenance contractor has a contract to paint lines on the highways and county roads for the county. It needs to paint lines on 500 miles of roads once every 6 years. It needs to paint a double white line down the center of all 500 miles of the roads. On 200 miles of these roads, it also needs to paint a single yellow line on the left-side of the road. How many miles of yellow and white lines will the company need to paint over the next 12 years?
A) 700
B) 900
C) 1400
D) 2400

112) Which of the following is the greatest?
A) 0.540
B) 0.054
C) 0.045
D) 0.5045

113) A blacksmith makes iron railings for homes and exteriors. The railings are made in 1/16 inch increments in diameter. The blacksmith has just made a railing that is 5/8 inch diameter, but he has realized that it is too large for the current project. What size diameter should he try next?
A) 9/16
B) 11/16
C) 13/16
D) 3/4

114) An accessories store can buy 12 pairs of gloves for $10 in total. Individual pairs of gloves cost $1.50 per pair. What is the best price the store will pay if it buys 15 pairs of gloves?
A) $10.00
B) $11.50
C) $13.60
D) $14.50

115) A supervisor performs safety checks on children's car seats and booster seats. The number of units that do not pass the safety inspection each day must be reported. A report of the results for the week is shown below. What is the approximate mean amount of units that have passed inspection for the five days?

Row	Hour	Units Produced	Passed Inspection	Failed Inspection
1	Monday	980	968	12
2	Tuesday	823	817	6
3	Wednesday	954	942	12
4	Thursday	1036	1018	18
5	Friday	890	879	11

A) 879
B) 921
C) 925
D) 942

116) A store that sell appliances can purchase 120 washing machines from its usual supplier for $172 each. The store can get the same 120 washing machines from a second supplier for $20,500 in total or from a third supplier for $19,000 plus 7% sales tax. How much will the store pay to get the best deal?
A) $19,000
B) $20,330
C) $20,500
D) $20,640

117) A store that sells wallets, purses, and bags can buy one style of bag for $4 and sell it for $12. The store uses the same percentage mark up on a second style of bag that it buys for $3. What figure below represents the price of the second style of bag?
A) $9
B) $10
C) $11
D) $12

118) The price of an item is normally $22.50, but customers with a membership can purchase it at the discounted price of $20. What percentage best represents the membership discount?
A) 0.125%
B) 12.5%
C) 0.111%
D) 11%

119) An online business received the following scores from a customer satisfaction survey: 9.8; 8.7; 9.5; 7.9; 8.6; 6.3; 9.9; 5.4. What is the average of these scores?
A) 8.2625
B) 8.65
C) 9.4
D) 66.10

120) A is 3 times B, and B is 3 more than 6 times C. Which of the following describes the relationship between A and C?
A) A is 9 more than 18 times C.
B) A is 3 more than 3 times C.
C) A is 3 more than 18 times C.
D) A is 6 more than 3 times C.

121) A store paid $217 for an item of inventory. This included 8.5% sales tax. What was the price of the item before tax?
A) $198.56
B) $200.00
C) $208.50
D) $235.45

122) A business has received $123 off an order. This amounted to a 40% discount off the original price. How much would the business have paid without the discount?
A) $30.75
B) $49.20
C) $205.00
D) $307.50

123) A hairdressing salon provides haircuts, styling, and other services to customers. The manicurist has reported that it takes 5 hours to do 4 full manicures and 2.5 hours to do 5 full pedicures. How long should it take the manicurist to do 20 full manicures and 25 full pedicures?
   A) 7 hours and 30 minutes
   B) 12 hours and 30 minutes
   C) 37 hours and 50 minutes
   D) 37 hours and 30 minutes

124) A librarian for a local community college has prepared a recent report on a publishing project which shows that shows that 57.75% of the project has been completed in the past 7 work days. If work continues at the same rate, approximately how many work days will be required in total for the entire project?
   A) 9
   B) 10
   C) 12
   D) 14

125) A veterinary practice is trying to find the best deal on some veterinary supplies. The practice wants to purchase 135 units of a certain feline medication. One company charges $15.30 per unit, plus 6% sales tax. Another company charges $2,100 for the whole order plus a $75 administration charge, but does not charge sales tax. If the practice chooses the best price, how much will it pay for the medication?
   A) $2,065.50
   B) $2,100.00
   C) $2,175.00
   D) $2,189.43

126) A liquid ingredient is stored in 5-quart containers. There are two partially-full containers, one with $4^3/_8$ quarts and another with $3^7/_8$ quarts. How many quarts are there in total in these two containers?
   A) $1^1/_4$
   B) 7
   C) $7^1/_8$
   D) $8^1/_4$

127) If $7x$ is between 5 and 6, which of the following could be the value of x?
   A) $^2/_3$
   B) $^3/_4$
   C) $^5/_8$
   D) $^7/_8$

Measurement and Data

Note that formulas and conversions are provided in the appendix at the end of the book.

128) A student receives the following scores on her assignments during the term:
98.5, 85.5, 80.0, 97, 93, 92.5, 93, 87, 88, 82
What is the range of her scores?
A) 17.0
B) 18.0
C) 18.5
D) 89.65

129) A manufacturing company makes beverages for select retailers. 3 quarts and 2 cups of flavoring are needed for the first batch of the day, and 4 quarts and 3 cups of flavoring are needed for the second batch. How much flavoring is needed for both batches in total?
A) 2 gallons and 1 cup
B) 1 gallon and 1 cup
C) 8 quarts and 2 cups
D) 7 quarts and 4 cups

130) A cartographer must calculate the distance between cities in her state. She has measured a distance between two cities of 38 miles. What is the approximate distance between the cities in terms of kilometers?
A) 24
B) 61
C) 125
D) 3800

131) A company that supplies food products to caterers buys tomato sauce by the crate. A crate containing 100 cans of tomato sauce weighs 90 pounds and 12 ounces. The crate weighs 15 pounds when it is empty. Each can of tomato sauce weighs 12 ounces. Approximately how many cans of tomato sauce are in the crate?
A) 101
B) 121
C) 139
D) 1200

132) A company in your local area sells different types of rope. The rope comes in coiled bundles that are labeled with the number of feet in each bundle. The company needs to change the labels so that they show the length of each one in millimeters. What formula should be used?
A) millimeters = feet × 0.3048
B) millimeters = feet × 0.3048 × 1,000
C) millimeters = feet ÷ 0.3048
D) millimeters = feet × 0.3048 ÷ 1,000

133) A climatologist needs to calculate the mean high temperature in one city over a five-day period in degrees Celsius. However, the high temperatures are reported in Fahrenheit. The following data has been collected: Day 1: 72° F; Day 2: 68° F; Day 3: 65° F; Day 4: 82° F; Day 5: 81° F. What was the approximate mean high temperature in degrees Celsius?
A) 71°C
B) 23°C
C) 74°C
D) 32°C

134) A rectangular vegetable garden has an area of 360 square feet. If the length of the garden is 30 feet, what is the width of the garden?
A) 12 feet
B) 24 feet
C) 115 feet
D) 150 feet

135) A building contractor is laying wooden parquet pieces on a floor. The floor is 8 feet long by 4 feet wide. Each wooden parquet piece measures 12 inches by 6 inches. What is the minimum number of wooden parquet pieces that will be needed in order to cover the wooden part of the floor?
A) 16
B) 32
C) 48
D) 64

136) A painter is painting a wall that is 16 feet long and 11 feet high. She needs to calculate the surface area of the wall in order to know how much paint to buy. What is the surface area of the wall in square feet?
A) 54
B) 121
C) 176
D) 256

137) A rectangular solid container needs to be filled with a liquid substance. The length of the rectangular solid is 12 feet, the width is 9 feet, and the volume is 1080 cubic feet. What is the height of the rectangular solid?
A) 10 feet
B) 12 feet
C) 90 feet
D) 100 feet

138) A beaker is cylindrical and measures 18 inches high and 12 inches in diameter. However, the volume has to be converted from cubic inches to gallons for a report. What is the approximate volume of the beaker in terms of gallons?
A) 2.9 gallons
B) 8.8 gallons
C) 10.4 gallons
D) 8,138.88 gallons

139) The volume of a cube-shaped object needs to be calculated. The cube has a side length of 9 feet. However, a report is asking for the volume of the object in terms of cubic inches. Which figure below should be used?
A) 729 cubic inches
B) 1,728 cubic inches
C) 139,968 cubic inches
D) 1,259,712 cubic inches

140) A company ships products overseas in large rectangular shipping containers. One type of container is 25 feet long, 12 feet wide, and 18 feet high. The container is currently 75% full of a particular product. What is the volume of the product in the container?
A) 150 cubic feet
B) 200 cubic feet
C) 405 cubic feet
D) 4,050 cubic feet

141) A company manufactures glue and other adhesives that contain a chemical called PVA. At least 50 quarts of PVA need to be in stock at the start of every month. Inventory has been taken this morning and there are 2 containers of PVA that hold 16 cups and 7 ounces each. There are also 3 containers of PVA that hold 20 cups and 4 ounces each. This PVA must be purchased in 5-quart containers. How many containers are needed in order to replenish the stock?
A) 0
B) 5
C) 6
D) 7

142) A company that manufactures hand soap and laundry detergent has to order liquid parabens that are used in its products. The parabens are stored in two identically sized vats. The vats measure 10 feet by 10 feet by 12 feet. The first vat is $^3/_4$ full and the second vat is $^4/_5$ full. The parabens cost 12 cents a cubic inch. To the nearest dollar, what is the cost value of the parabens in the two vats?
A) $223
B) $3,857
C) $4,977
D) $385,690

143) A company that manufactures batteries stores acid in a conical-shaped container that is 6 feet in diameter and 8 feet in height. What is the volume of the container in cubic feet?
A) 48.00
B) 75.36
C) 113.04
D) 226.08

144) An electrician installs wiring and lighting in new homes. The client would like to install lights on the walls in the living room. The living room is 25 feet long and 10 feet wide. The client would like a light to be installed on each wall in 5-foot increments. However, no lights are to be installed in the corners of the room. How many lights will be needed in order to carry out this job?
A) 8
B) 10
C) 12
D) 14

145) A company that manufactures ice cubes and frozen refreshments makes two sizes of ice cubes. The large ice cubes have a side length of 1.8 millimeters, and the small ice cubes have a side length of 1.4 millimeters. What is the amount in cubic millimeters of the difference in volume between the large ice cube and the small one?
A) 0.064
B) 1.960
C) 2.744
D) 3.088

146) A building engineer has been asked to calculate the areas of two triangular shapes. The large triangle has a base of 12 inches and a height of 18 inches. The small triangle has a base of 8 inches and a height of 14 inches. What is the difference in the areas of the two shapes?
A) 8
B) 16
C) 25
D) 52

Look at the table below and answer questions 147 to 150.

Disease or Complication	Percentage of patients with this disease that have survived and total number of patients
Cardiopulmonary and vascular	82% (602,000)
HIV/AIDS	73% (215,000)
Diabetes	89% (793,000)
Cancer and leukemia	48% (231,000)
Premature birth complications	64% (68,000)

147) Approximately how many patients with diabetes have survived?
A) 58,050
B) 87,230
C) 156,950
D) 705,770

148) The highest number of deaths occurred as a result of which disease?
A) Cardiovascular an pulmonary disease
B) HIV/AIDS
C) Cancer and leukemia
D) Premature birth complications

149) Approximately how many cancer and leukemia patients have not survived?
A) 24,500
B) 110,900
C) 120,000
D) 231,000

150) Which of the following statements is supported by the data?
A) Most people with cancer and leukemia have survived.
B) The percentage of people dying from HIV/AIDS is less than it was in the past.
C) If a patient at the hospital was selected at random, there would be an 82% chance that he or she suffers from cardiopulmonary or vascular disease.
D) Diabetes patients had a greater chance of survival than patients with other diseases or complications.

151) An online magazine business charges a $59 subscription fee for every customer who signs up during the week. This week, 14 customers signed up. How much did the business make on upfront subscription fees for these customers this week?
A) $726
B) $762
C) $826
D) $862

152) Packaging weight changes for the first three years of business were as follows. Year 1: −92 grams; Year 2: 35 grams; Year 3: −16 grams. What figure below represents the change in the packaging weight from year 1 to year 2?
A) −57
B) 57
C) 19
D) 127

153) The ages of 5 siblings are: 2, 5, 7, 12, and x. If the average age of the 5 siblings is 8 years old, what is the age (x) of the 5th sibling?
A) 8
B) 10
C) 12
D) 14

154) 75.00 milliliters of medication were on hand at the beginning of the month and 8.35 milliliters have been dispensed. How many milliliters of the medication are left?
A) 66.65
B) 66.75
C) 65.65
D) 66.55

155) Mark's record of times for the 400 meter freestyle at swim meets this season is:
8.19, 7.59, 8.25, 7.35, 9.10
What is the median of his times?
A) 7.59
B) 8.19
C) 8.25
D) 8.096

156) An auto shop does custom paint and vinyl wrap jobs on vintage cars. An employee worked 7.5 hours each day for 2 days on a job for one customer. The customer was billed $75 per hour for the employee's work, and the employee was paid $40 per hour. How much money did the shop make for the work on this job after paying the employee's wages?
A) $262.50
B) $300.00
C) $525.00
D) $600.00

157) The following numbers are ordered from least to greatest: α, $^2/_7$, $^8/_9$, 1.35, $^{11}/_3$, μ
Which of the following could be the value of μ?
A) 3.5
B) $^{10}/_4$
C) 4.1
D) $^1/_6$

158) A small factory uses tarpaulin to make covers for farm implements. There was $12^7/_{16}$ yards of tarpaulin at the start of the day. At the end of the day, $8^9/_{16}$ yards of tarpaulin is left. Which amount below represents the amount of tarpaulin used this day in yards?
A) $2^{14}/_{16}$
B) $3^1/_8$
C) $3^7/_8$
D) $4^7/_8$

159) Abdul purchased 80 items for sale, and he has sold 0.75 of them in relation to the total purchased. How many items does he have left after making these sales?
A) 10 items
B) 20 items
C) 25 items
D) 40 items

160) For a particular sugar-craft product, 3 parts of icing sugar must be added to every 6 parts of sugar paste. A batch of sugar-craft that has 14 parts of sugar paste is being prepared. How many parts of icing sugar should be added to this batch?
A) 3
B) 6
C) 7
D) 8

161) In a shipment of 100 mp3 players, 1% of the mp3 players are faulty. What is the ratio of non-faulty mp3 players to faulty mp3 players?
A) 99:1
B) 1:100
C) 100:1
D) 1:99

162) A cell phone is purchased at a cost of x and sold at four times the cost. Which of the following represents the profit on each of these cell phones?
A) x
B) $3x$
C) $4x$
D) $3 - x$

163) Galvanized pipe is manufactured in 1/64 inch increments in diameter. You have selected a pipe that is 23/64 inch diameter, but have realized that it is too large for your current project. What size diameter should you try next?
A) 1/4
B) 11/32
C) 12/32
D) 13/32

164) A footwear store can purchase 325 pairs of tennis shoes from its normal supplier for $4 a pair. It can get the same 325 pairs of shoes from a second supplier for $1,250 plus 6% sales tax, or from a third supplier for $1,290. How much will the store pay to get the best deal?
A) $1,250.00
B) $1,290.00
C) $1,300.00
D) $1,367.40

165) A customer paid $344.50 for her purchase, which included 6% sales tax. What was the price of the item before tax?
A) $323.83
B) $325.00
C) $333.90
D) $343.44

166) Find the value of x that satisfies the following inequality: $-|26 - 54| \le |5 + x|$
A) $x \ge 23$
B) $x \ge 75$
C) Any real number.
D) No real number.

167) Which of the following is the value below rounded to the nearest hundredth?
95,324.8716
A) 95,300.0000
B) 95,324.9000
C) 95,324.8700
D) 95,324.8720

168) Which of the following shows the numbers ordered from least to greatest?
A) 0.2135
   0.3152
   0.0253
   0.0012

B) 0.3152
   0.2135
   0.0253
   0.0012

C) 0.0253
   0.0012
   0.3152
   0.2135

D) 0.0012
   0.0253
   0.2135
   0.3152

169) Mr. Rodriguez teaches a class of 25 students. Ten of the students in his class participate in drama club. In which graph below does the dark gray area represent the percentage of students who participate in drama club?

A)

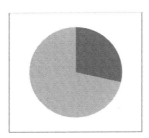

B)

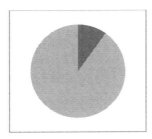

C)

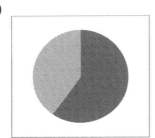

D)

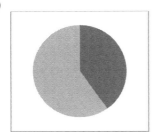

170) The graph below shows the relationship between the number of days of rain per month and the amount of people who exercise outdoors per month. Which statement is supported by the data?

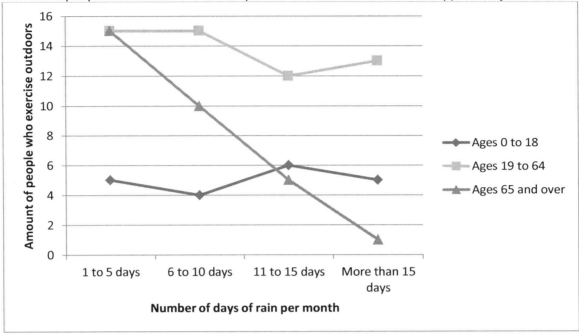

A) Young children are reliant upon an adult in order to exercise outdoors.
B) The exercise habits of working age people seem to fluctuate proportionately to the amount of rainfall.
C) In the 19 to 64 age group, there is a negative relationship between the number of days of rain and the amount of people who exercise outdoors.
D) People aged 65 and over seem less inclined to exercise outdoors when there is more rain.

171) A textile manufacturing company can buy cloth for $3 a meter from an overseas supplier. However, the cost of the cloth needs to be reported in inches for the company's financial statements. How many inches of cloth can be purchased for $3?
A) 2.54
B) 3.937
C) 39.37
D) 100

172) Angle A of a triangle measures 36°. Angles B and C have the same measurement each in degrees. What is the measurement of angle B?
A) 36°
B) 45°
C) 72°
D) 144°

173) A football field is 100 yards long and 30 yards wide. What is the area of the football field in square yards?
A) 3000
B) 1500
C) 300
D) 260

174) A small pasture has a length of 5 yards and a width of 3 yards. Barbed wire will be placed on all four sides of the outside of this pasture. How many yards of barbed wire should be ordered?
   A) 15
   B) 16
   C) 18
   D) 40

175) A circular ornament has a diameter of 12. Which formula should be used to calculate the circumference of the ornament?
   A) 6 × 3.14
   B) 12 × 3.14
   C) 24 × 3.14
   D) 36 × 3.14

176) A box is manufactured to contain either laptop computers or notebook computers. When the computer systems are removed from the box, it is reused to hold other items. If the length of the box is 20 centimeters (cm), the width is 15cm, and the height is 25cm, what is the volume of the box in cubic centimeters?
   A) 150
   B) 300
   C) 750
   D) 7500

177) What is the mode of the numbers in the following list?
   1.6, 2.9, 4.5, 2.5, 2.5, 5.1, 5.4
   A) 3.5
   B) 3.1
   C) 3.0
   D) 2.5

178) An individual tire-and-rim product weighs 32 pounds and 4 ounces. The product is loaded into a wooden crate, and the crate when empty weighs 60 pounds. Each individual rim weighs 19 pounds. The crate when completely full to capacity weighs 447 pounds. How many units can each crate contain?
   A) 11
   B) 12
   C) 13
   D) 14

179) The legend for a map states that 1 inch on the map is equal to 20 miles in actual distance. There is a space of 2 and a half inches between two cities on the map. What figure below best represents the actual distance in kilometers between these two cities?
   A) 31.06
   B) 32.2
   C) 80.5
   D) 322

180) A company is making its budget for the cost of employees to attend conferences for the year. It costs $7,500 per year in total for the company plus C dollars per employee. During the year, the company has E employees. If the company has budgeted $65,000 for conference attendance, which equation can be used to calculate the maximum cost per employee?
A) ($65,000 − $7,500) ÷ E
B) ($65,000 − $7,500) ÷ C
C) (C − $7,500) ÷ E
D) $65,000 ÷ E

181) If $2(3x - 1) = 4(x + 1) - 3$, what is the value of x?
A) $x = {}^{3}/_{2}$
B) $x = {}^{2}/_{3}$
C) $x = {}^{4}/_{3}$
D) $x = {}^{3}/_{4}$

Look at the diagram below and answer questions 182 and 183.

Brooke wants to put new flooring in her living room. She will buy the flooring in square pieces that measure 1 square foot each. The entire room is 8 feet by 12 feet. The bookcases are two feet deep from front to back. Flooring will not be put under the bookcases. Each piece of flooring costs $5.50. A diagram of her living room is provided.

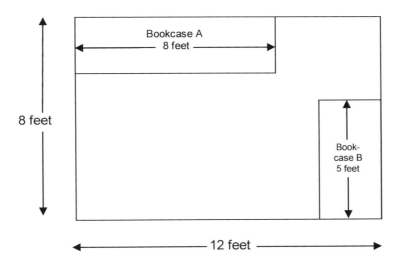

182) How much will Brooke pay to cover her living room floor?
A) $350
B) $385
C) $480
D) $528

183) If Brooke gets a 27.5% discount off the $5.50 price per tile, about how much will she pay to cover her living room floor?
A) $105
B) $255
C) $280
D) $382

184) Which of the following shows the numbers ordered from greatest to least?
A) $-\frac{1}{3}$, $\frac{1}{7}$, 1 , $\frac{1}{5}$
B) $-\frac{1}{3}$, $\frac{1}{5}$, $\frac{1}{7}$, 1
C) $-\frac{1}{3}$, 1 , $\frac{1}{7}$, $\frac{1}{5}$
D) 1 , $\frac{1}{5}$, $\frac{1}{7}$, $-\frac{1}{3}$

185) If $3x - 9 = -18$, then $x = $?
A) -6
B) 6
C) -3
D) 3

186) Evaluate: $2x^2 + 8x$ if $x = 7$
A) 154
B) 105
C) 98
D) 56

187) An art and craft store received $7,375 for sales of a certain type of scrapbook this year. If these scrapbooks were sold for $59 each, how many of them were sold this year?
A) 135
B) 125
C) 120
D) 75

188) Consider the inequality: $-3x + 14 < 5$
Which of the following values of x is a possible solution to the inequality above?
A) −3.1
B) 2.25
C) 2.65
D) 4.35

189) $^6/_{25}$ of the inventory has been sold this month. Approximately what percentage of the inventory has been sold?
A) 0.24%
B) 2.40%
C) 24.0%
D) 4.167%

190) Changes to monthly cash flow is reported as a decimal figure, which is calculated by dividing the net change in cash flow into the previous month's cash flow. Last month, the change to cash flow was 0.40. What percentage best represents the change to cash flow for last month?
A) 0.40%
B) 4.00%
C) 40.0%
D) 400%

191) The temperature on Saturday was 62°F at 5:00 PM and 38°F at 11:00 PM. If the temperature fell at a constant rate on Saturday, what was the temperature at 9:00 PM?
A) 58°F
B) 54°F
C) 50°F
D) 46°F

192) Hot dogs sell for $2.50 each, and hamburgers sell for $4 each. A family went out to eat and bought 3 hamburgers. They also bought hot dogs. The total cost of their food was $22. How many hot dogs did they buy?
A) 2
B) 3
C) 4
D) 5

193) Which of the following shows the numbers ordered from least to greatest?
A) $-^1/_4$, $^1/_8$, $^1/_6$, 1
B) $-^1/_4$, $^1/_8$, 1 , $^1/_6$
C) $-^1/_4$, $^1/_6$, $^1/_8$, 1
D) $-^1/_4$, 1 , $^1/_8$, $^1/_6$

194) Which number is correctly rounded?
A) 32.81 to the tenths place is 32.9
B) 10.0005 to the thousandths place is 10.001
C) 5.468 to the hundredths place is 5.46
D) 291,489 to the hundreds is 291,000

195) When rounded to the nearest whole number, which of the following best estimates
(53.1 + 9.912)/6.4?
A) (53 + 10)/6
B) (53 + 10)/7
C) (53 + 9)/6
D) (54 + 10)/6

196) Which of the following equations is equivalent to $\frac{x}{5} + \frac{y}{2}$?

A) $\frac{x+y}{7}$

B) $\frac{2x+5y}{10}$

C) $\frac{5x+2y}{10}$

D) $\frac{5y}{2x}$

197) Solve for x : $3x - 2(x + 5) = -8$
A) 1
B) 2
C) 3
D) 5

198) A painter needs to paint 8 rooms, each of which has a surface area of 2000 square feet. If one bucket of paint covers 900 square feet, what is the fewest number of buckets of paint that must be purchased to complete all 8 rooms?
A) 3
B) 17
C) 18
D) 19

199) Soon Li jogged 3.6 miles in $^3/_4$ of an hour. What was her average jogging speed in miles per hour?
A) 4.8
B) 4.6
C) 4.2
D) 2.7

200) The price of a certain book is reduced from $60 to $45 at the end of the semester. By what percent is the price of the book reduced?
A) 15%
B) 20%
C) 25%
D) 33%

201) The ratio of males to females in the senior year class of Carson Heights High School was 6 to 7. If the total number of students in the class was 117, how many males were in the class?
A) 48
B) 54
C) 56
D) 58

202) The table below shows the relationship between the total number of chicken sandwiches a customer can buy and the total price for each order. If a customer takes the deal that has the lowest price per sandwich, what will the customer pay per sandwich?
2 chicken sandwiches for $17.50
4 chicken sandwiches for $34.40
8 chicken sandwiches for $68.00
A) $4.00
B) $8.00
C) $8.50
D) $9.50

203) A pizzeria sold 15 cheese pizzas, 10 pepperoni pizzas, and 5 vegetable pizzas one day. Cheese pizzas sell for $10 each; pepperoni pizzas sell for $12, and the total sales of all three types of pizza for that day was $310. What price is charged for 1 vegetable pizza?
A) $5
B) $8
C) $9
D) $10

204) Shanika works as a car salesperson. She earns $1,000 a month in basic pay, plus $390 for each car she sells. If she wants to earn at least $4,000 this month, what is the minimum number of cars that she must sell this month?
A) 6
B) 7
C) 8
D) 9

205) One private airplane flew at a constant speed, traveling 780 miles in 2 hours. How many miles did this plane travel in the last 40 minutes of its journey?
A) 120
B) 180
C) 200
D) 260

206) A horse ran 12 furlongs in 2 minutes and 48 seconds. Assuming that the same amount of time was spent on each furlong, how many seconds does it take the horse to run one furlong?
A) 0.014 seconds
B) 0.14 seconds
C) 1.40 seconds
D) 14 seconds

207) A national report states that 30 out of every 100 television viewers watch TV for more than 25 hours her week. If there are 3,200 television viewers in Newtown, how many television viewers in Newtown watch TV for more than 25 hours per week?
A) 320
B) 750
C) 960
D) 1,067

208) An item costs $22 each if the customer collects it in person from the store, and an extra $3 for postage and handling is charged per item if the customer wants the item sent by courier. This week, 32 customers purchased this item and requested that the item be sent by courier. How much money in total did the store make on the items sold to these 32 customers?
A) $800
B) $704
C) $575
D) $96

209) $107^3/_8$ yards of adhesive plastic is needed to complete one work order and $96^1/_8$ yards of adhesive plastic is needed for another work order. How many yards of adhesive plastic is needed in total in order to complete both of these work orders?
A) $193^1/_8$
B) $203^1/_2$
C) $193^1/_4$
D) $203^1/_4$

210) A vat contains 163.75 units of red colorant, 107.50 units of blue colorant, 91.25 units of yellow colorant, and 10.30 units of black colorant. Which of the following represents, in terms of units, how full the vat is after these 4 colorants have been placed in it?
A) 362.50
B) 371.50
C) 372.80
D) 373.50

211) A customer who owns a small hotel has ordered 10 new quilts. Each quilt requires 2 yards of red fabric for the front, 1 yard of blue fabric for the front, and a further 3 yards of blue fabric for the back. The quilts need to have an embellishment in gold, and a total amount of 6 yards of gold fabric is needed to make the embellishments for all 5 quilts. Each quilt also has edging in white, and half a yard of white material is needed for the edging for each quilt. How many yards of fabric in total will be needed to complete this order?
A) 7.7
B) 77
C) 3.85
D) 38.5

212) Members of a weight loss group report their individual weight loss to the group leader every week. During the week, the following amounts in pounds were reported: 1, 1, 3, 2, 4, 3, 1, 2, and 1. What is the mode of the weight loss for the group?
A) 1 pound
B) 2 pounds
C) 3 pounds
D) 4 pounds

Look at the diagram below and answer question 213.

A packaging company secures their packages with plastic strapping prior to shipment. The box is 20 inches in height, 22 inches in depth, and twenty 42 inches in length. For certain packages, 15 extra inches of strapping is used to make a handle on the top of the package to carry it. The strapping is wrapped around the length and width of the entire package, as shown in the following diagram:

213) How many inches of strapping is needed for one package, including making the handle?
A) 124
B) 128
C) 252
D) 267

214) Fence panels are going to be placed along one side of a field. Each panel is 8 feet 6 inches long. 11 panels are needed to cover the entire side of the field. How long is the field?
A) 60 feet 6 inches
B) 72 feet 8 inches
C) 93 feet 6 inches
D) 102 feet 8 inches

215) The area of a square floor is 64 square units. The floor needs to be covered entirely with tiles. Each floor tile is 4 square units. How many tiles are needed to cover the floor?
A) 8
B) 12
C) 16
D) 24

216) The base of a cylinder is at a right angle to its sides. The radius of the base of the cylinder measures 5 centimeters. The height of the cylinder is 10 centimeters. What is the volume of this container in cubic centimeters?
A) 785
B) 157
C) 78.5
D) 31.4

217) Cone A has a base radius of 9 and a height of 18. Cone B has a base radius of 3 and a height of 6. Which number below expresses the ratio of the volume of Cone A to Cone B?
A) 27
B) $^1/_{27}$
C) 3
D) $^1/_6$

Look at the graph below and answer question 218.

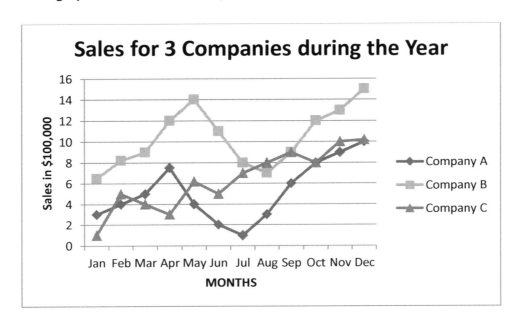

218) Consider only the data for July to December. Then choose the statement below that is best supported by the data.
A) Sales increased every month for Company A.
B) Sales increased every month for Company B.
C) Sales increased every month for Company C.
D) Sales increased every month for all three companies.

219) $6 + \frac{x}{4} \geq 22$, then $x \geq$?
A) −8
B) 64
C) −64
D) 128

220) The residents of Hendersonville took a census. As part of the census, each resident had to indicate how many relatives they had living within a ten-mile radius of the town. The results of that particular question on the census are represented in the graph below.

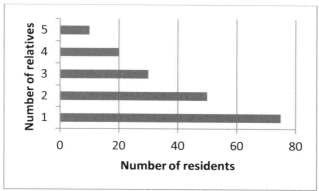

How many residents of Hendersonville had more than 3 relatives living within a ten-mile radius of the town?
A) 10
B) 20
C) 30
D) 155

Look at the information below and answer question 221.

Chantelle took a test that had four parts. The total number of questions on each part is given in the table below, as is the number of questions that Chantelle answered correctly.

Part	Total Number of Questions	Number of Questions Answered Correctly
1	15	12
2	25	20
3	35	32
4	45	32

221) What was Chantelle's percentage score of correct answers for the entire test?
A) 75%
B) 80%
C) 86%
D) 90%

Look at the pie chart below and answer question 222.

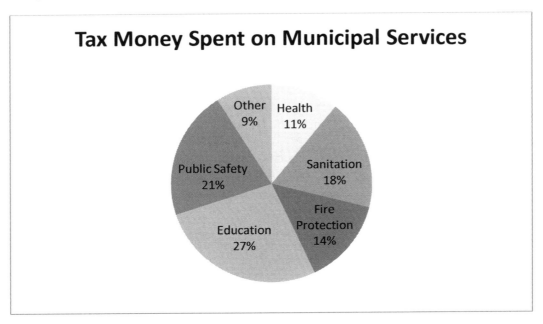

Tax Money Spent on Municipal Services

Other 9%
Health 11%
Public Safety 21%
Sanitation 18%
Fire Protection 14%
Education 27%

222) If $5,275,300 in total tax money was spend on all municipal services, how much was spend on education?
A) $474,777
B) $580,283
C) $1,107,813
D) $1,424,331

223) A store sells domestic cleaning products. A certain type of liquid cleaner is sold in increments of 1/4 of a cup. Each 1/4 of a cup costs 50 cents. One customer buys $10^1/_4$ cups of this cleaner. How much will she pay for this purchase?
A) $5.13
B) $5.50
C) $10.50
D) $20.50

224) Find the equivalent of 6 yards in inches.
A) 18 inches
B) 72 inches
C) 216 inches
D) 1,296 inches

225) 4 out of every 5 employee-satisfaction questionnaires have been completed and returned. If a company has 250 total employees, and every employee must complete and return the questionnaire, how many questionnaires have not been completed and returned?
A) 4
B) 5
C) 50
D) 200

226) A flower store sells poinsettia plants for $20 during December and for $12 during January. In December, 55 customers purchased poinsettias, and 20 customers purchased them in January. How much money did the store receive for poinsettia sales during December and January?
A) $240
B) $1,060
C) $1,100
D) $1,340

227) During each flight, a flight attendant is required to count the number of passengers on board the aircraft. The morning flight had 52 passengers more than the evening flight, and there were 540 passengers in total on the two flights that day. How many passengers were there on the evening flight?
A) 244
B) 296
C) 488
D) 540

228) 110 students took a math test. The mean score for the 60 female students was 95, while the mean score for the 50 male students was 90. Which figure below best approximates the mean test score for all 110 students in the class?
A) 55
B) 90
C) 92.5
D) 92.73

229) A caterpillar travels 10.5 inches in 45 seconds. How far will it travel in 6 minutes?
   A) 45 inches
   B) 63 inches
   C) 64 inches
   D) 84 inches

230) Each week, a company tabulates the results of customer satisfaction surveys by region and calculates the bonuses to be paid. The company has four regions, each of which has one salesperson. Salespeople in each region receive bonuses based on the amount of positive customer feedback they receive. The results of the surveys were as follows:
   Region 1: 40 positive customer feedback results
   Region 2: 30 positive customer feedback results
   Region 3: 20 positive customer feedback results
   Region 4: 30 positive customer feedback results
   If the four salespeople received $540 in bonuses in total, how much bonus money does the company pay each individual salesperson per satisfied customer?
   A) $4.00
   B) $4.50
   C) $4.90
   D) $5.00

231) A plumber charges $100 per job, plus $25 per hour worked. He is going to do 5 jobs this month. He will earn a total of $4,000. How many hours will he work this month?
   A) 10
   B) 40
   C) 80
   D) 140

232) The students at Lyndon High School have been asked about their plans to attend the Homecoming Dance. The chart below shows the responses of each grade level by percentages. Which figure below best approximates the percentage of the total number of students from all four grades who will attend the dance? Note that each grade level has roughly the same number of students.

	Will Attend	Will Not Attend	Undecided
Freshmen:	45%	24%	31%
Sophomores:	30%	45%	25%
Juniors:	38%	20%	42%
Seniors:	30%	25%	45%

   A) 25%
   B) 35%
   C) 45%
   D) 55%

233) An employment agency for temporary employees charges clients $15 per hour for each hour the temporary employee works. The agency pays each temporary employee $12 an hour and retains the difference as a commission. The agency had 10 employees who worked 40 hours each this week. How much did the agency make on commission for these 10 employees this week?
   A) $30.00
   B) $120.00
   C) $1,200.00
   D) $4,800.00

234) 49 out of the 50 items in a company's product line had above average sales this month. What percentage of the items in the product line had above average sales this month?
A) 0.098%
B) 0.98%
C) 9.80%
D) 98%

235) A fabric store sells ribbon in 3-inch or one-foot increments. One customer wanted two types of ribbon, and she bought $8^3/_4$ feet of one type of ribbon and $7^1/_2$ feet of another type. How much ribbon did this customer buy in total?
A) 7 feet and 6 inches
B) 8 feet and 9 inches
C) 15 feet and 3 inches
D) 16 feet and 3 inches

236) Hours spent on a work order are recorded by the tenth of an hour in 6 minute increments. For a particular work order, $28^3/_{10}$ hours in total have been budgeted. $7^9/_{10}$ hours have already been spent on the work order. Which amount below represents the amount of time left for this work order?
A) $36^1/_5$
B) $35^6/_{10}$
C) $20^2/_5$
D) $20^3/_5$

237) A decorative stone mix requires 2 parts of white gravel for every 3 parts of blue slate chippings. An order requires 147 parts of blue slate chippings. How many parts of white gravel should be added?
A) 73.5
B) 88.0
C) 98.0
D) 220.5

238) A baseball team sells T-shirts and sweatpants to the public for a fundraising event. The total amount of money the team earned from these sales was $850. Variable t represents the number of T-shirts sold and variable s represents the number of sweatpants sold. The total sales in dollars is represented by the equation $25t + 30s$. What equation represents the fraction of the amount earned by selling sweatpants to the total amount earned?
A) $s/850$
B) $30s/850$
C) $(25t + 30s)/850$
D) $t/850$

239) An automotive store can buy a case containing 24 bottles of motor oil for $50 a case wholesale. Individual bottles of this brand of motor oil cost $2.50 per bottle wholesale. What is the best price the store will pay if it buys 100 bottles of motor oil wholesale?
A) $200.00
B) $200.10
C) $202.50
D) $210.00

240) Flavored rice cakes sold in the United States are measured in ounces, and units sold overseas are measured in grams. 39 ounces of flavoring are needed for a batch of rice cakes for the United States and 1,190.7 grams of the same flavoring are needed for another batch of rice cakes to be sold overseas. How much flavoring is needed for both batches in total?
A) 81 ounces
B) 40.48 ounces
C) 43.38 grams
D) 2,297.35 grams

241) A ceiling is 25 feet wide and 35 feet long. The ceiling is to be covered with square ceiling tiles that measure 6 inches by 6 inches each. How many of these square ceiling tiles are needed to install this ceiling?
A) 1,750
B) 3,500
C) 480
D) 875

242) This month, a nurse dispensed 1,275,000 milligrams of medication to patients. How many grams of medication were dispensed?
A) 127.5
B) 1,275
C) 12,750
D) 127,500,000

243) A basketball has a diameter of 10 inches. Which figure below best represents the volumetric capacity of the basketball in cubic inches?
A) 32
B) 523
C) 3,376
D) 8,576

244) Cell phone covers are sold for a retail price of $12 per unit. This amounts to a 525% markup over the cost for each unit. How much does each unit cost?
A) $0.192
B) $1.92
C) $6.25
D) $0.75

245) The perimeter of a rectangle is 350 feet and the width of the shortest side is 75 feet. What is the measurement of the length of the rectangle?
A) 10 feet
B) 90 feet
C) 95 feet
D) 100 feet

246) Storage boxes for rice flour measure 3 feet by 3 feet by 2 feet each. The first box is $\frac{1}{6}$ full, the second box is $\frac{1}{2}$ full, and the third box is $\frac{2}{3}$ full. A factory wants to replenish its supply of rice flour so that it will have three full boxes. The rice flour costs $9 a cubic foot. To the nearest dollar, what will it cost to replenish the stock in the three boxes?
A) $270
B) $466
C) $998
D) $4,666

247) A group of families had the following household incomes on their tax returns: $65000, $52000, $125000, $89000, $36000, $84000, $31000, $135000, $74000, and $87000. What is the range?
A) 74000
B) 77800
C) 79000
D) 104000

248) When 205,346.9781 is divided by 1,000, which digit of the resulting number is in the hundreds place?
A) 0
B) 2
C) 4
D) 6

249) Which of the following is equivalent to the expression $36 - 2x$ for all values of x?
A) $6 + 2(15 - x)$
B) $6(6 - 2x)$
C) $39 - (3 - 2x)$
D) $8(5 - 2x) - 4$

250) Find the equivalent: $-|-63 + 17|$
A) -46
B) 46
C) -80
D) 80

Look at the diagram and information below and answer question 251.

Each square in the diagram below is one yard wide and one yard long. The gray area of the diagram represents New Town's water reservoir. The white area represents the surrounding conservation park.

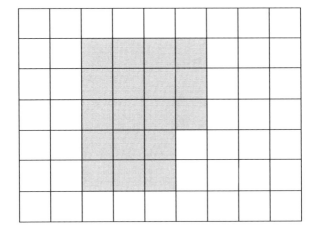

251) Which of the following ratios represents the area of the reservoir to the area of the surrounding conservation park?
A) 2:5
B) 9:23
C) 17:32
D) 18:44

252) Consider the scatterplot below and then choose statement that is best supported by the data.

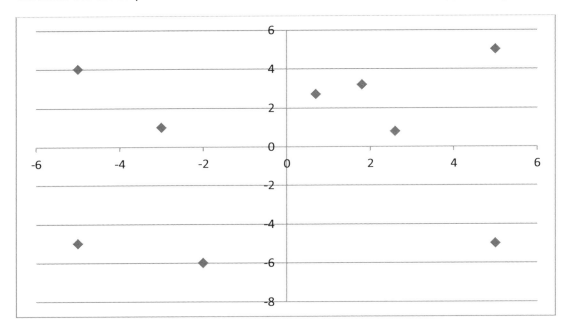

A) The scatterplot suggests a strong positive linear relationship.
B) The scatterplot suggests a strong negative linear relationship.
C) The scatterplot suggests a weak positive linear relationship.
D) No relationship can be discerned from the scatterplot.

Look at the bar chart below and answer question 253.

The chart below shows data on the number of vehicles involved in accidents in Cedar Valley.

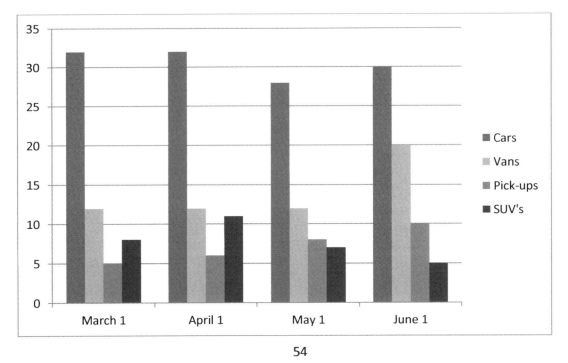

253) Which of the following statements is correct according to the data above?
   A) Cars accounted for the largest amount of total accidents for the four months.
   B) Vans accounted for the largest amount of total accidents for the four months.
   C) Pick-ups accounted for the largest amount of total accidents for the four months.
   D) SUV's accounted for the largest amount of total accidents for the four months.

254) Evaluate: $x^2 - 5x - 9$ if $x = 8$
   A) 5
   B) 15
   C) 40
   D) 64

255) Solve for x: $5x - 9 = 6$
   A) 3
   B) 6
   C) 8
   D) 9

256) Which of the following steps will solve the equation for x: $18 = 3(x + 5)$
   A) Subtract 5 from each side of the equation, and then divide both sides by 3.
   B) Subtract 18 from each side of the equation, and then divide both sides by 5.
   C) Multiply both x and 5 by 3 on the right side of the equation. Then subtract 15 from each side of the equation.
   D) Divide each side of the equation by 3. Then subtract 5 from both sides of the equation.

257) Which of the following values of x is a possible solution to the inequality?: $-3x + 14 < 5$
   A) −3.1
   B) 2.80
   C) 2.25
   D) 3.15

258) $20 - \dfrac{3x}{4} \geq 17$, then $x \leq ?$
   A) −12
   B) −4
   C) −3
   D) 4

55

259) Return on investment (ROI) percentages are provided for seven companies. The ROI will be negative if the company operated at a loss, but the ROI will be a positive value if the company operated at a profit. The ROI's for the seven companies were: –2%, 5%, 7.5%, 14%, 17%, 1.3%, –3%. Which figure below best approximates the mean ROI for the seven companies?
A) 2%
B) 5.7%
C) 6.25%
D) 7.5%

260) A salesperson gets $1,250 basic pay per month plus a $12 commission every time a customer orders more than $100 worth of products. This month, the salesperson had 32 customers who ordered more than $100 worth of products. How much did the salesperson earn in total this month?
A) $866
B) $1262
C) $1634
D) $1643

261) A farm store received $310 for sales insecticide. If this insecticide is sold for $12.40 each, how many of them did the store sell this month?
A) 6
B) 25
C) 38
D) 52

262) The ratio of bags of apples to bags of oranges in a store is 2 to 3. If there are 44 bags of apples in the store, how many bags of oranges are there?
A) 33
B) 48
C) 55
D) 66

263) A dance academy had 300 students at the beginning of January. It lost 5% of its students during the month. However, 15 new students joined the academy on the last day of the month. If this pattern continues for the next two months, how many students will there be at the academy at the end of March?
A) 285
B) 300
C) 310
D) 315

264) The price of a wool coat is reduced 12.5% at the end of the winter. If the original price of the coat was $120, what will the price be after the reduction?
A) $108.00
B) $107.50
C) $105.70
D) $105.00

265) A factory produces 20 times as many functioning microchips than defective chips. If the factory produced 11,235 chips in total last week, how many of them were defective?
A) 535
B) 561
C) 1,070
D) 10,700

266) The fine for speeding violations is $50 per violation. The fine for other violations is $20 per violation. This week, there were 60 speeding violations, 30 parking violations, and 90 other violations. The total collected for all three types of violations was $6,000. What is the fine for each parking violation?
A) $20
B) $30
C) $40
D) $100

267) The price of a sofa at a furniture store was x dollars on Wednesday this week. On Thursday, the price of the sofa was reduced by 10% of Wednesday's price. On Friday, the price of the sofa was reduced again by 15% of Thursday's price. Which of the following expressions can be used to calculate the price of the sofa on Friday?
A) $(0.75)x$
B) $(0.90)(0.85)x$
C) $(0.10)(0.15)x$
D) $(0.10)(0.85)x$

268) There are three boys in a family, named Alex, Burt, and Zander. Alex is twice as old as Burt, and Burt is one year older than three times the age of Zander. Which of the following statements best describes the relationship between the ages of the boys?
A) Alex is 4 years older than 6 times the age of Zander.
B) Alex is 2 years older than 6 times the age of Zander.
C) Alex is 4 years older than 3 times the age of Zander.
D) Alex is 2 years older than 3 times the age of Zander.

269) An accountant had two projects to complete for one particular client this month. She spent $37^2/_5$ hours on the first project and $25^4/_5$ hours on the other project. How many hours did she spend on projects for this client this month?
A) $63^1/_5$
B) $62^1/_5$
C) $53^1/_5$
D) $52^1/_5$

270) Research indicates that the best customer to sales-clerk ratio for high-end luxury stores is 3 to 1. A particular store is expecting 15 customers tomorrow. How many sales clerks should it have available?
A) 1
B) 3
C) 5
D) 12

271) It took from 9:15 AM to 10:25 AM for a painter to paint 7 square yards. The painter has to paint 17.5 square yards in total for this particular job. If he continues working at the same pace, what time will he finish painting?
A) 11:10 AM
B) 11:10 PM
C) 11:30 AM
D) 12:10 PM

272) 1235.35 units of product A, 567.55 units of product B, and 347.25 units of product C are needed for the order that is currently being processed. Which of the following represents the total number of units for all of the products in this order?
A) 2150.15
B) 2149.15
C) 1802.90
D) 1582.60

273) Soft drink is purchased for resale in 20 gallon containers. A store has one container with $19^3/_4$ gallons and another with $14^3/_4$ gallons of soft drink. How much soft drink does the store have in total in these two containers?
A) 5
B) $33^1/_2$
C) $33^3/_4$
D) $34^1/_2$

274) A company that manufactures aluminum products started the month with $102^7/_{18}$ yards of aluminum sheeting. $24^{11}/_{18}$ yards of aluminum sheeting was left at the end of the month. Which figure below represents the amount of aluminum sheeting used this month in yards?
A) $77^7/_9$
B) $78^7/_9$
C) $77^2/_9$
D) $78^2/_9$

275) Four items are going to be placed in a box. The items have the following weights in pounds: 5.14, 4.98, 3.20, 8.78. The box itself weighs 1 pound. What is the best estimate of the total weight of the parcel when the items are placed inside the box?
A) 22
B) 23
C) 28
D) 30

276) The radius of circle A is 5 centimeters. The radius of circle B is 3 centimeters. Which of the following statements is true?
A) The difference between the areas of the circles is approximately 6.28.
B) The difference between the areas of the circles is approximately 28.26.
C) The difference between the circumferences of the circles is approximately 6.28.
D) The difference between the circumferences of the circles is approximately 12.56.

277) A rectangle has a length of 18 inches and a width of 10 inches. What is the perimeter of the rectangle in inches?
A) 36
B) 46
C) 56
D) 180

278) The circumference of the floor space of a circular arena is approximately 1,017.36 feet. A partition needs to be placed in the middle of the floor space in order to create two equal semi-circular parts. What is the measurement in feet of the partition?
A) 6
B) 18
C) 108
D) 324

279) Product A normally costs $20 per unit. With a membership card, a $4 discount per unit is given. The store has started to offer the same percentage discount on Product B. Product B normally costs $16 per unit. What figure below represents the purchase cost of Product B after the discount?
A) $3.20
B) $4.00
C) $12.00
D) $12.80

280) A rectangular-shaped container has a side length of 10 inches, a height of 7 inches, and a width of 5 inches. Which figure below best approximates the volume of the container in cubic inches?
A) 1.52
B) 152
C) 350
D) 80,850

281) A herbal therapy product comes as a liquid that needs to be diluted with organic wheat grass juice. To get the correct concentration, 3 ounces of herbal therapy product has to be added to every 2 cups of organic wheat grass juice that is used. A mixture that contains 14 cups of organic wheat grass juice needs to be made. How many ounces of herbal therapy product should be added to the juice to get the correct concentration for this batch of product?
A) 6
B) 7
C) 11
D) 21

282) There are 10 cars in a parking lot. Nine of the cars are 2, 3, 4, 5, 6, 7, 9, 10, and 12 years old, respectively. If the average age of the 10 cars is 6 years old, how old is the 10th car?
A) 1 year old
B) 2 years old
C) 3 years old
D) 4 years old

283) At an elementary school, 3 out of ten students are taking an art class. If the school has 650 students in total, how many total students are taking an art class?
A) 65
B) 130
C) 195
D) 217

284) Mustafa bought 4 quarts of cranberry juice for $3 per quart and x quarts of orange juice for $2 per quart. He paid $18 for his entire purchase. How many quarts of orange juice did he buy?
A) 5
B) 4
C) 3
D) 2

285) 5 more than 4 times the number x is equal to the number y.
Which statement below represents this equation?
A) 5x + 4 = y
B) 4x + 5 = y
C) 4(x + 5) = y
D) 4(y + 5) = x

Look at the information below and answer question 286.

A recipe of the ingredients needed to make 4 brownies is provided below.

Brownie recipe

¼ cup of flour
½ cup of sugar
¼ cup of butter
3 tablespoons of cocoa powder
¼ teaspoon of baking powder
½ teaspoon of vanilla extract

286) How much vanilla extract is needed to make 6 brownies?
A) ¼ teaspoon
B) ¾ teaspoon
C) 1¼ teaspoons
D) 1½ teaspoons

287) $-|5 - 8|$ = ?
A) −13
B) 13
C) −3
D) 3

288) If $\frac{1}{5}x + 3 = 5$, then x = ?

A) $\frac{8}{5}$

B) $-\frac{8}{5}$

C) 8

D) 10

289) In Brown County Elementary School, parents are advised to have their children vaccinated against five childhood diseases. Which one of the following statements is supported by the data?

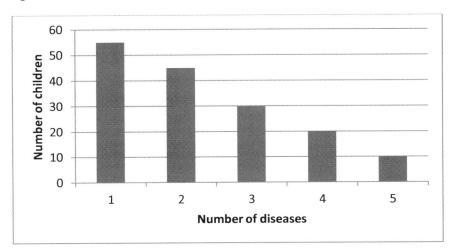

A) 30 children were vaccinated against at least three diseases
B) 90 children were vaccinated against at least two diseases
C) 60 children were vaccinated against at least three diseases.
D) 110 children were vaccinated against at least four diseases

290) In a group of children, one-half have had a tetanus shot. Of that half, only one-third suffered wounds that would have caused tetanus. In which of the following graphs does the dark gray area represent that third of the group?

A)

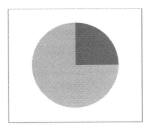

B)

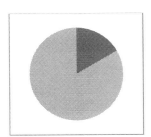

C)

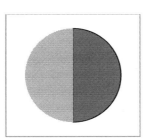

D)

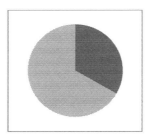

291) Which of the following dimensions would be needed in order to find the area of the figure?

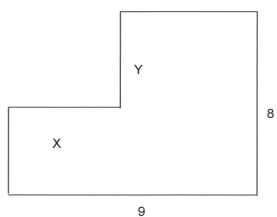

A) X only
B) Y only
C) Both X and Y
D) Either X or Y

292) The triangle in the illustration below is an equilateral triangle. What is the measurement in degrees of angle a?

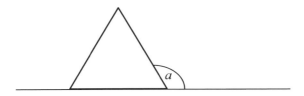

A) 40
B) 45
C) 60
D) 120

293) A farmer has a rectangular pen in which he keeps animals. He has decided to divide the pen into two parts. To divide the pen, he will erect a fence diagonally from the two corners, as shown in the diagram below. How long in yards is the diagonal fence?

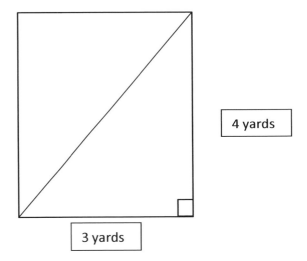

4 yards

3 yards

A) 4
B) 5
C) 5.5
D) 6

294)   ∠XYZ is an isosceles triangle, where XY is equal to YZ. Angle Y is 30° and points W, X, and Z are co-linear. What is the measurement of ∠WXY?

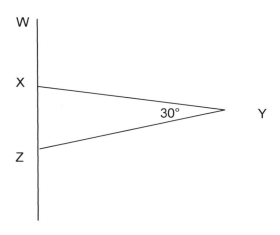

A) 40
B) 105
C) 150
D) 160

295) A business has already achieved $^9/_{16}$ of its projected sales for this year. Approximately what percentage of the projected sales have already been achieved?
A) 0.5625%
B) 5.625%
C) 56.25%
D) 43.75%

296) Which one of the following statements is best supported by the data below?

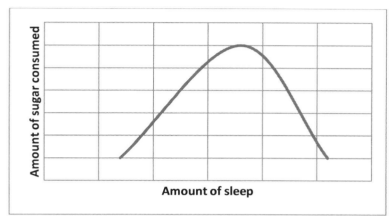

A) For certain quantities of sugar consumption, there is only a 50% chance of being correct when trying to predict the amount of sleep a person will get.
B) Sugar appears to make a person sleep more up to a point, but too much sugar will have the opposite effect.
C) There is a positive relationship between the amount of sugar a person consumes and the amount of sleep he or she gets.
D) There is an inverse relationship between the amount of sugar a person consumes and the amount of sleep he or she gets.

297) Which of the following is the value below rounded to the nearest tenth?
473.862
A) 470.00
B) 473.80
C) 473.90
D) 473.86

298) Employee loss rate is calculated by dividing the number of employees who left a company during the year into the total number of employees in the company at the start of the year. You had 120 employees at the start of the year, and your employee loss rate was 0.05 for the year. How many employees do you have at the end of the year?
A) 119
B) 114
C) 12
D) 6

299) A furniture store that sells tables, chairs, and other types of furniture has given a 20 percent discount this month on one of the tables that it sells. This amounts to a discount of $60. What was the original price of the table?
A) $80
B) $120
C) $1200
D) $300

300) An ice cream store orders ice cream in 10-quart containers. At the start of the day on Wednesday, there were $6^3/_4$ quarts of praline nut ice. At the close of business that Wednesday, there were $2^1/_2$ quarts of praline nut ice cream left. How much praline nut ice cream was sold that day?
A) $4^1/_4$
B) $4^3/_8$
C) $4^5/_8$
D) $4^6/_8$

301) 9 ounces of liquid need to be added to every 6 ounces of active chemical. The current job lot requires 10 ounces of active chemical. How many ounces of liquid should be added?
A) 1.50
B) 15.0
C) 0.67
D) 67.0

302) Susan wanted to find the mean of the six surveys she administered this month. However, she erroneously divided the total points from the six surveys by 5, which gave her a result of 96. What is the correct mean of her six surveys?
A) 63
B) 80
C) 82
D) 91

303) A bakery makes brownies, cakes, and other confections every day. It allows employees to take home the goods that have not sold by the close of business each day. There are 3 partial trays of unsold brownies at the end of the day, and each tray has $^1/_8$ of the brownies left in it. These brownies need to be divided among four employees. What amount below represents the fraction of a tray of brownies that each employee will receive?
A) $^1/_6$
B) $^{32}/_3$
C) $^3/_{32}$
D) $^3/_{24}$

304) This month Person A lost $14^3/_4$ pounds, Person B lost $20^1/_5$ pounds, and Person C lost 36.35 pounds. What is the total weight loss for these three people?
A) 71.30
B) 71.05
C) 71.15
D) 71.25

305) An office purchased 50 reams of paper this month. At the end of the month, 5 of these reams of paper have been used. Which decimal figure below best expresses the amount of reams of paper that have been used in relation to the amount of reams that were purchased?
A) 0.0010
B) 0.0100
C) 0.1000
D) 0.0500

306) One hundred prospective candidates took an aptitude test for a new job opening. The 55 female candidates had an average score of 87, while the 45 male candidates had an average of 80. What was the average aptitude test score for all 100 candidates?
A) 82.00
B) 83.15
C) 83.50
D) 83.85

307) Mary works for a charity and needs to get $650 in donations. So far, she has obtained 80% of the money she needs. How much money does she still need?
A) $130.00
B) $13.00
C) $32.50
D) $81.85

308) The Abdul family is shopping at a superstore. They buy product A and product B. Product A costs $5 each, and product B costs $8 each. They buy 4 of product A. They also buy a certain quantity of product B. The total value of their purchase is $60. How many units of product B did they buy?
A) 4
B) 5
C) 6
D) 8

309) The price of socks is $2 per pair and the price of shoes is $25 per pair. Anna went shopping for socks and shoes, and she paid $85 in total. In this purchase, she bought 3 pairs of shoes. How many pairs of socks did she buy?
A) 2
B) 3
C) 5
D) 8

310) Chain-link fence is sold by the 1/2 yard. Each 1/2 yard sells for $10.50. One customer buys $20\frac{1}{2}$ yards of this particular type of fence. How much will the customer pay for this purchase?
A) $215.25
B) $225.75
C) $430.50
D) $450.50

311) $49\frac{3}{16}$ inches of rope is needed to finish one job and $18\frac{1}{16}$ inches is needed for another. How many inches of rope are needed in order to complete both jobs?
A) $66\frac{1}{8}$
B) $67\frac{1}{8}$
C) $66\frac{1}{4}$
D) $67\frac{1}{4}$

312) 11 out of 132 SIM cards are defective. What percentage best represents the amount of defective SIM cards in relation to the total?
A) 0.08%
B) 8%
C) 83%
D) 92%

313) To make soda-bread biscuits, the best proportion of baking soda to flour is 2 to 9. A batch of soda-bread biscuits calls for 126 cups of flour. How many cups of baking soda should be used?
A) 28
B) 18
C) 14
D) 7

314) Marsha worked from 12:10 PM to 2:25 PM knitting 3 caps by hand from alpaca yarn. At this rate, how many caps will she knit during a 9-hour period?
A) 6
B) 12
C) 36
D) 27

315) The graph below shows the relationship between the amount of hours students spent studying for an exam out of 70 available hours and the resulting number of incorrect answers students had on the exam out of 100 possible questions. Which one of the following statements is best supported by the data?

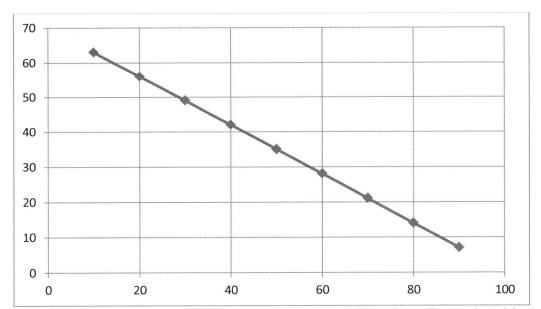

A) The graph can be used to predict the number of hours a student will spend studying.
B) A student's exam performance can be predicted based upon the number of hours he or she spends studying.
C) There is a positive relationship between the amount of incorrect answers and the number of hours a student spends studying.
D) There is an inverse relationship between the amount of incorrect answers and the number of hours a student spends studying.

316) If a circle has a radius of 4, what equation can be used to calculate the circumference of the circle?
   A) 3.14 ÷ 8
   B) 3.14 ÷ 16
   C) 8 × 3.14
   D) 16 × 3.14

317) If a circle has a radius of 6, what equation can be used to calculate the area of the circle?
   A) 6 × 3.14
   B) 12 × 3.14
   C) 24 × 3.14
   D) 36 × 3.14

318) If circle A has a radius of 0.4 and circle B has a radius of 0.2, what is the difference in area between the two circles?
   A) 0.1256
   B) 0.3768
   C) 0.5024
   D) 1.256

319) A rectangular box has a base that is 5 inches wide and 6 inches long. The height of the box is 10 inches. What is the volume of the box in cubic inches?
   A) 30
   B) 110
   C) 150
   D) 300

320) Find the area of the right triangle whose base is 2 and height is 5.
   A) 2.5
   B) 5
   C) 10
   D) 15

321) Find the approximate volume of a cone which has a radius of 3 and a height of 4.
   A) 12.56
   B) 37.68
   C) 4.1762
   D) 2.355

322) Pat wants to put wooden trim around the floor of her family room. Each piece of wood is 1 foot in length. The room is rectangular and is 12 feet long and 10 feet wide. How many pieces of wood does Pat need for the entire perimeter of the room?
   A) 22
   B) 44
   C) 100
   D) 120

323) A circular pond has a diameter of 36 feet. What figure below best approximates the area of the pond?
   A) 1017
   B) 804
   C) 113
   D) 57

324) A student receives the following scores on his exams during the semester:

89, 65, 75, 68, 82, 74, 86

What is the mean of his scores?

A) 24
B) 74
C) 75
D) 77

325) What is the median of the numbers in the following list?:

2.5, 9.4, 3.1, 1.7, 3.2, 8.2, 4.5, 6.4, 7.8

A) 3.2
B) 4.5
C) 5.2
D) 6.4

326) Evaluate: $2x^2 - x + 5$ if $x = -2$

A) 8
B) 13
C) 15
D) 20

327) Solve for x: $-6x + 5 = -19$

A) 4
B) 6
C) 8
D) 12

328) If $2(3x - 1) = 4(x + 1) - 3$, what is the value of x?

A) $^3/_2$
B) 3
C) $^2/_3$
D) 2

Look at the bar chart below and answer question 329.

An athlete ran 10 miles in 1.5 hours. The graph below shows the miles the athlete ran every 10 minutes.

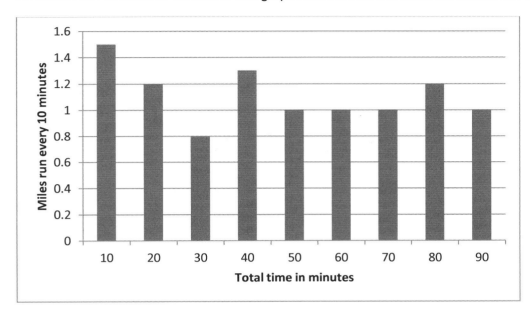

329) According to the graph, about how many miles did the athlete run in the first 30 minutes?
   A) 0.8 miles
   B) 2.0 miles
   C) 3.0 miles
   D) 3.5 miles

330) Find the value of x that satisfies the following inequality: $125 - |-94 + 107| \leq x$
   A) x ≤ 112
   B) x ≥ 112
   C) x ≤ 326
   D) x ≤ 326

ATI TEAS Practice Problems 1 to 80 – Solutions and Explanations

1) The correct answer is C. The problem is asking for the total for all three years, so we add the three figures together: $25,135 + $32,787 + $47,004 = $104,926

2) The correct answer is D. For questions that ask you to calculate the change given to a customer, you need to take the amount of money the customer gives the cashier and subtract the amount of the purchase: $50.00 – $41.28 = $8.72

3) The correct answer is D. Multiplication problems will often include the words 'each' or 'every.' The problem states that the salesperson earns a $175 referral fee on every customer, so the referral fee was earned 8 times this month. We need to multiply the amount of the referral fee by the number of customers to solve: $175 × 8 = $1400

4) The correct answer is C. Division problems will often include the word 'per.' The problem states that the employee works 30 hours per week. So, we divide the total weekly amount by the number of hours to solve: $535.50 ÷ 30 = $17.85

5) The correct answer is B. When you have to add a negative number to a positive number, you are really subtracting. So, add the business profits and subtract the business losses:
953 + 1502 – 286 – 107 = 2062

6) The correct answer is A. In this problem, we need to subtract the excess of the depth of Lake Bajo from the location below sea level of Lake Alto. The location below sea level of Lake Alto is a negative number, so we subtract as follows: –35 – 62 = –97. Remember to express your result as a negative number.

7) The correct answer is B. In order to express a fraction as a decimal, treat the line in the fraction as the division symbol: 3/5 = 3 ÷ 5 = 0.60. Be careful with the decimal placement in your final result.

8) The correct answer is C. To express a decimal number as a percent, move the decimal point two places to the right and add the percent sign: 0.55 = 55.0%

9) The correct answer is D. In order to express a fraction as a percentage, you need to divide and then express the result as a percentage. Step 1 – Treat the line in the fraction as the division symbol: 5/14 = 5 ÷ 14 = 0.357. Step 2 – To express the result from Step 1 as a percentage, we need to move the decimal point two places to the right and add the percent sign: 0.357 = 35.7%

10) The correct answer is D. For your exam, you should be able to recognize the equivalent fractions for commonly-used decimal numbers. If you are unsure, perform division on the answer choices to check:
3/4 = 3 ÷ 4 = 0.75

11) The correct answer is A. For your exam, you should be able to recognize the equivalent fractions for commonly-used percentages. If you are unsure, perform division on the answer choices to check:
1/3 = 1 ÷ 3 = 0.3333 = 33%

12) The correct answer is C. Any given percentage is out of 100%, so we divide by 100 to express a percentage as a decimal. So, move the decimal point two places to the left and remove the percent sign: 45% = 45 ÷ 100 = 0.45

13) The correct answer is B. Express both amounts as decimal numbers and multiply to solve: $14^1/_4$ pounds × 36 cents per pound = 14.25 × 0.36 = $5.13

14) The correct answer is C. There are 60 minutes in an hour, so multiply the minutes in the hour by the decimal number given in the problem to solve: 60 minutes × 0.35 hour = 60 × 0.35 = 21 minutes

15) The correct answer is A. Step 1 – Subtract the discount from the original price: $24 – $5 = $19. Step 2 – Take the result from Step 1 and multiply by the number of units sold: $19 × 12 = $228

16) The correct answer is D. Step 1 – Determine the total number of hours worked: 7 hours per day for 4 days = 7 × 4 = 28 hours. Step 2 – Calculate the profit the company makes per hour. The customer was billed $45 per hour for the employee's work, and he was paid $25 per hour: $45 – $25 = $20 profit per hour. Step 3 – Multiply the total number of hours by the profit per hour to solve: 28 hours × $20 profit per hour 28 × 20 = $560

17) The correct answer is A. Step 1 – Calculate how many minutes there are in 40 hours: 40 hours × 60 minutes per hour = 2400 minutes. Step 2 – Divide the amount of prescriptions into the previous result to get the rate: 2400 ÷ 250 = 9.6 minutes per prescription

18) The correct answer is C. The orders that were delivered on time are part of the total order. So, take the amount of orders that were delivered on time and divide by the amount of total orders: 105 ÷ 120 = 0.875 = 87.5%

19) The correct answer is B. On Monday cell growth was 27, and for all of the days Tuesday through Friday, cell attrition was 13 per day. Step 1 – Cell attrition is a negative number, so perform multiplication to get the total for the four days (Tuesday through Friday): –13 × 4 = –52. Step 2 – On Monday cell growth was 27, so add this to the result from Step 1 to solve: –52 + 27 = –25

20) The correct answer is B. To find the average, you need to find the total, and then divide the total by the number of hours. Step 1 – Find the total: 23 + 25 + 26 + 24 + 22 = 120. Step 2 – Divide the result from Step 1 by the number of hours: 120 ÷ 5 = 24

21) The correct answer is D. Step 1 – Take the 66 units of cement powder for the current batch and divide by the 3 units stated in the original ratio: 22 ÷ 3 = 22. Step 2 – Multiply the result from Step 1 by the 2 units of sand stated in the original ratio to get your answer: 2 × 22 = 44

22) The correct answer is D. The problem states that we are working with a ratio, so the employees and the supervisors form separate groups. Step 1 – Add the two groups together: 50 + 1 = 51. Step 2 – Take the total amount of employees stated in the problem and divide this by the figure calculated in Step 1 to get the amount of supervisors: 255 ÷ 51 = 5

23) The correct answer is D. The problem uses the phrase '2 out of every 20 employees' so we know that there are 2 employees who form a subset within each group of 20. Step 1 – Take the total number of

employees and divide this by 20: 480 ÷ 20 = 24. Step 2 – Take the result from Step 1 and multiply by the amount in the subset to solve: 24 × 2 = 48

24) The correct answer is C. Step 1 – Calculate the amount of time spent on the initial job to do 3 wheel covers: 8:10 to 8:22 = 12 minutes. Step 2 – Calculate how many minutes are needed to change 1 wheel cover: 12 minutes ÷ 3 = 4 minutes each. Step 3 – Divide the figure from Step 2 into 60 minutes to solve: 60 ÷ 4 = 15

25) The correct answer is C. Step 1 – Add the whole numbers. The whole numbers are the numbers in front of the fractions: 15 + 13 = 28. Step 2 – Add the fractions. If you have two fractions that have the same denominator, you add the numerators and keep the common denominator: 2/8 + 5/8 = 7/8. Step 3 – Combine the results from Step 1 and Step 2 to get your new mixed number to solve the problem: 28 + 7/8 = $28^7/_8$

26) The correct answer is A. Step 1 – Add the whole numbers: 2 + 4 = 6. Step 2 – Add the fractions. If you have two fractions that have the same denominator, you add the numerators and keep the common denominator: 1/8 + 3/8 = 4/8. Step 3 – Simplify the fraction from Step 2: 4/8 = (4 ÷ 4)/(8 ÷ 4) = 1/2. Step 4 – Combine the results from Step 1 and Step 3 to get your new mixed number to solve the problem: 6 + 1/2 = $6^1/_2$

27) The correct answer is A. Step 1 – Subtract the whole numbers: 5 – 4 = 1. Step 2 – Subtract the fractions. If you have two fractions that have the same denominator, you subtract the numerators and keep the common denominator: 3/16 – 1/16 = 2/16. Step 3 – Simplify the fraction from Step 2: 2/16 = (2 ÷ 2)/(16 ÷ 2) = 1/8. Step 4 – Combine the results from Step 1 and Step 3 to get your new mixed number to solve the problem: 1 + 1/8 = $1^1/_8$

28) The correct answer is B. Add the three figures together to solve: 0.25 + 0.50 + 0.10 = 0.85. Remember to be sure to put the decimal point in the correct place when you work out the solution to problems like this one.

29) The correct answer is C. Add the percentages together to solve: 25% + 50% = 75%

30) The correct answer is D. Step 1 – Multiply the whole numbers: 5 × 1 = 5. Step 2 – Multiply the whole number by the fraction: 5 × 1/4 = 5/4. Step 3 – Convert the fraction from Step 2 to a mixed number: 5/4 = $1^1/_4$. Step 4 – Combine the results from Step 1 and Step 3 to get your new mixed number: 5 + $1^1/_4$ = $6^1/_4$. Step 5 – Convert the result from Step 4 to hours and minutes: $6^1/_4$ hours = 6 hours and 15 minutes

31) The correct answer is B. Step 1 – Convert the first fraction to the common denominator: 1/8 = (1 × 4)/(8 × 4) = 4/32. Step 2 – Add one more increment to this to get your result: 4/32 + 1/32 = 5/32

32) The correct answer is A. Step 1 – Work out the cost for the first supplier: 50 units × $0.50 = $25. Step 2 – Compare to other deals to solve: The other deals are $27.50 and $30, so $25 is the best deal.

33) The correct answer is D. Step 1 – Determine the duration of the stay in weeks and nights: 9 nights = 1 week + 2 nights. Step 2 – Add the cost for 1 week to the cost for 2 days to solve: $280 + (2 × $45) = $280 + $90 = $370

34) The correct answer is D. Step 1 – Determine the dollar value of the discount: $15 – $12 = $3.
Step 2 – Divide the result from Step 1 by the original price to get the percentage: $3 ÷ $15 = 0.20 = 20%

35) The correct answer is C. Step 1 – Determine the dollar value of the markup on the mug: $9 retail price – $3 cost = $6 markup. Step 2 – Calculate the percentage of the markup by dividing the dollar value of the markup by the cost: $6 ÷ $3 = 2.00 = 200%. Step 3 – Use the percentage markup from the previous step to determine the dollar value of the markup on the bowl: $4 × 200% = $4 × 2 = $8. Step 4 – Add the dollar value of the markup for the bowl to the cost of the bowl to get the retail price: $8 + $4 = $12

36) The correct answer is D. To calculate a reverse percentage you need to divide, rather than multiply. So, take the $20 discount and divide by the 25% percentage: $20 ÷ 25% = $20 ÷ 0.25 = $80

37) The correct answer is D. For problems that ask you to find the largest possible product of two even integers, first you need to divide the sum by 2. The sum in this problem is 22, so divide by 2. 22 ÷ 2 = 11 Now take the result from this division and find the 2 nearest even integers that are 1 number higher and lower.
11 + 1 = 12
11 − 1 = 10
Then multiply these two numbers together in order to get the product: 12 × 10 = 120

38) The correct answer is C. Step 1 – Determine the cost from the first supplier: 240 × 0.25 = $60. The tax on this will be $60 × 6.5% = $60 × 0.065 = $3.90. Then add the tax to the cost to get the total: $60 + $3.90 = $63.90. Step 2 – Determine the total cost from the second supplier: $58 cost + ($58 × 0.065 tax) = $58 + 3.77 = $61.77. So, you will get the better deal from the second supplier at $61.77.

39) The correct answer is D. Step 1 – Determine how many days are needed to make the small frames. 20 small frames can be made in 4 days: 20 frames ÷ 4 days = 5 small frames per day. The customer wants 40 small frames, so divide by the rate to determine how many days are going to be needed for the small frames: 40 frames ÷ 5 per day = 8 days. Step 2 – Determine how many days are going to be needed to make the large frames. 21 larges frames can be made in 3 days: 21 ÷ 3 = 7 large frames per day. 64 large frames need to be made for the order: 64 ÷ 7 = 9.1 days. Step 3 – Add the results from the two previous steps to solve: 8 days + 9.1 days = 17.1 days, which we round down to 17 days.

40) The correct answer is C. Step 1 – Calculate the percentage of work completed per day. 12.5% of the work has been completed in 4 days: 12.5 % ÷ 4 days = 3.125% per day. Step 2 – Determine how many days in total are needed to complete the entire job by dividing 100% by the result from the previous step: 100% ÷ 3.125% = 32 days. Step 3 – Determine the number of days remaining: 32 days in total – 4 days completed = 28 days remaining

41) The correct answer is B. Perform the division, and then check the decimal places of the numbers. Divide as follows: 1523.48 ÷ 100 = 15.2348. Reading our result from left to right: 1 is in the tens place, 5 is in the ones place, 2 is in the tenths place, 3 is in the hundredths place, 4 is in the thousandths place, and 8 is in the ten-thousandths place.

42) The correct answer is C. The problem states that the volume of item A is 15 units less than 5 times the volume of item B. So set up your equation based on each part of the question: 5 times the volume of item B = 5B. The volume of A is 15 less than 5 times the volume of item B, so A = 5B − 15

43) The correct answer is C. Substitute −2 for x to solve.
$2x^2 − x + 5 =$
$[2 × (−2^2)] − (−2) + 5 =$
$[2 × (4)] − (−2) + 5 =$
$(2 × 4) + 2 + 5 =$
$8 + 2 + 5 = 15$

44) The correct answer is B. Isolate x to solve. You do this by doing the same operation on each side of the equation.
$−6x + 5 = −19$
Subtract 5 from each side to get rid of the integer 5 on the left side.
$−6x + 5 − 5 = −19 − 5$
Then simplify.
$−6x = −24$
Then divide each side by −6 to isolate x.
$−6x ÷ −6 = −24 ÷ −6$
$x = −24 ÷ −6$
$x = 4$

45) The correct answer is B.
Remember to do multiplication on the items in parentheses first.
$4x − 3(x + 2) = −3$
$4x − 3x − 6 = −3$
Then deal with the integers.
$4x − 3x − 6 + 6 = −3 + 6$
$4x − 3x = 3$
Then solve for x.
$4x − 3x = 3$
$x = 3$

46) The correct answer is C. Isolate the integers to one side of the equation.

$$\frac{3}{4}x − 2 = 4$$

$$\frac{3}{4}x − 2 + 2 = 4 + 2$$

$$\frac{3}{4}x = 6$$

Then get rid of the fraction by multiplying both sides by the denominator.

$$\frac{3}{4}x × 4 = 6 × 4$$

$$3x = 24$$

Then divide to solve the problem.

$3x \div 3 = 24 \div 3$

$x = 8$

47) The correct answer is B. Substitute 1 for x: $\dfrac{x-3}{2-x} = \dfrac{1-3}{2-1} = (1-3) \div (2-1) = -2 \div 1 = -2$

48) The correct answer is A. First, Isolate the whole numbers.

$50 - \dfrac{3x}{5} \geq 41$

$(50 - 50) - \dfrac{3x}{5} \geq 41 - 50$

$-\dfrac{3x}{5} \geq -9$

Then get rid of the denominator on the fraction.

$-\dfrac{3x}{5} \geq -9$

$\left(5 \times -\dfrac{3x}{5}\right) \geq -9 \times 5$

$-3x \geq -9 \times 5$

$-3x \geq -45$

Then isolate the remaining whole numbers.

$-3x \geq -45$

$-3x \div 3 \geq -45 \div 3$

$-x \geq -45 \div 3$

$-x \geq -15$

Then deal with the negative number.

$-x \geq -15$

$-x + 15 \geq -15 + 15$

$-x + 15 \geq 0$

Finally, isolate the unknown variable as a positive number.

$-x + 15 \geq 0$

$-x + x + 15 \geq 0 + x$

$15 \geq x$

$x \leq 15$

49) The correct answer is B. $14 - 82 = -68$; and the absolute value of -68 is 68.

50) The correct answer is B. $|-47 + 35| = 12$, so we need the value of -12 for the inequality to equal zero. The value of -11 for x would give us a result equal to 1, which is greater than zero, so the statement $x \geq -12$ satisfies the inequality.

51) The correct answer is B. From the formula, we can see that 1 foot = 0.3048 meters. To solve, multiply the amount of 538 feet, stated in the question, by 0.3048: $538 \times 0.3048 = 163.98$, which we round up to 164.

52) The correct answer is D. Step 1 – Add the feet together: 123 + 138 = 261 feet. Step 2 – Add the inches together: 6 + 8 = 14 inches. Step 3 – Convert the inches to feet and inches if the result from Step 2 is 12 inches or more: 14 inches = 1 foot 2 inches. Step 4 – Combine the results from Step 1 and Step 3 to solve: 261 feet + 1 foot 2 inches = 262 feet 2 inches

53) The correct answer is A. Step 1 – Convert the weight of the full box from pounds and ounces to just ounces. We are using the formula 1 pound = 16 ounces, so 8 pounds and 5 ounces = (8 × 16) + 5 = 128 + 5 = 133 ounces. Step 2 – The problem states that the box weighs 7 ounces when it is empty. So, subtract the weight of the empty box from the weight of the full box to get the weight of the product inside the box: 133 ounces – 7 ounces = 126 ounces. Step 3 – The problem tells us that each supplement weighs 0.75 ounces. Take the total weight from the previous step and divide by the weight per unit to determine how many units the box contains: 126 ounces ÷ 0.75 ounces = 168 units

54) The correct answer is B. Step 1 – Convert the mixed numbers to decimals and then multiply: $50^1/_4$ feet × $60^1/_4$ feet = 50.25 × 60.25 = 3027.5625 square feet. Step 2 – The price is given in square yards, so convert the square feet from the previous step to square yards. The formula states that 1 square yard = 9 square feet, so 1/9 square yard = 1 square foot: 3027.5625 square feet ÷ 9 = 336.3958 square yards. Step 3 – Calculate the cost: 336.3958 × $5.25 = $1765.92, which we round to $1,766.

55) The correct answer is B. Step 1 – Calculate the amount of remaining stock in inches: (2 × 75 inches) + (4 × 25.25 inches) = 150 + 101 = 251 inches. Step 2 – Convert the existing stock from inches to yards: 1 foot = 12 inches and 1 yard = 3 feet, so there are 36 inches in 1 yard. So, divide the amount of inches by 36 to convert to yards: 251 ÷ 36 = 6.97 yards. Step 3 – Calculate the amount required to restock. 60 yards are required in total, and there are 6.97 yards on hand, so subtract to find out how many more yards are needed to get the stock back up to 60 yards: 60 – 6.97 = 53.03 yards needed. Step 4 – The yarn comes in 5-yard balls, so calculate how many balls to buy to cover the 53.03 yards that are required: 53.03 ÷ 5 = 10.6 balls. It is not possible to buy a fractional part of a ball, so we round up to 11 balls.

56) The correct answer is D. Step 1 – Convert 0.75 grams to milligrams. 1 gram = 1,000 milligrams, so 0.75 grams × 1,000 = 750 milligrams. Step 2 – The normal ratio is in the amount of 50 milligrams, so divide the result from the previous step by 50: 750 ÷ 50 = 15. So, 15 times more active ingredient is being used than normal. Step 3 – Determine the amount of liquid. Since 15 times more of the active ingredient is being used, we also need to use 15 times more of the liquid: 1.5 milliliters × 15 = 22.5 milliliters

57) The correct answer is B. From the formula, we can see that the area of a triangle is ½ (base × height). So, substitute the values to solve: ½ (base × height) = ½ (12 × 14) = ½ × 168 = 84 square inches

58) The correct answer is C. Use the Pythagorean Theorem to solve. $C = \sqrt{A^2 + B}$
$C = \sqrt{A^2 + B^2} = \sqrt{3^2 + 2^2} = \sqrt{9 + 4} = \sqrt{13}$

59) The correct answer is C. The sum of the angles in a triangle is 180 degrees. So, subtract the measurements of the other two angles to solve: 180° – 47° – 44° = 89°

60) The correct answer is D. From the tip after the question, we can see that a circle has 360 degrees. So, subtract to solve: 360 – 82 – 79 – 46 – 85 = 68

61) The correct answer is A. From the formula, we can see that the area of a circle ≈ 3.14 × (*radius*)^2. So, put in 12 feet for the radius to solve: 3.14 × (12 × 12) = 3.14 × 144 = 452.16

62) The correct answer is C. From the formula, we know that the circumference of a circle ≈ 3.14 × diameter. The problem states that the diameter of the tractor tire is 46.5 inches, so use that in the formula to solve: 3.14 × 46.5 = 146.01 inches

63) The correct answer is D. The area of a rectangle = length × width. Your quilt is 6 feet long and 5 feet wide, so multiply to solve: 6 × 5 = 30

64) The correct answer is B. The perimeter of a rectangle = 2(length + width). Your field is 12 yards long and 9 yards wide, so use the formula to solve: 2(12 + 9) = 2 × 21 = 42

65) The correct answer is B. Step 1 – The area of a circle ≈ 3.14 × radius^2. Here, we are given the area, so we have to divide by 3.14, instead of multiplying by 3.14, as stated in the formula: 78.5 ÷ 3.14 = 25. Step 2 – The result from the previous step is the radius squared. A squared number is the result of a number that has been multiplied by itself. 5 × 5 = 25, so the length of the radius of the pond is 5 feet. Step 3 – Remember that diameter is double the radius, so if the radius is 5, the diameter is 10 feet.

66) The correct answer is D. The volume of a rectangular solid = length × width × height. The tank is 5 feet wide, 8 feet long, and 3 feet high, so multiply to solve: 5 × 8 × 3 = 120

67) The correct answer is A. A cube is a three-dimensional object in which all sides have the same length. The volume of a cube = side length^3. So, put the length of the side in the formula to solve: 18 × 18 × 18 = 5832

68) The correct answer is A. Step 1 – Calculate in cubic inches the volume of the sphere when it is full. The tank is 72 inches across on the inside, so the radius is 36 inches. The volume of a sphere ≈ 4/3 × 3.14 × radius^3: 4/3 × 3.14 × 36^3 = 195,333.12 cubic inches. Step 2 – Calculate in cubic inches how much milk remains in the sphere. The tank is now 80% full of milk: 195,333.12 cubic inches × 0.80 = 156,266.50 cubic inches, which we round to 156,267 cubic inches.

69) The correct answer is B. The volume of a cylinder ≈ 3.14 × height × radius^2. Your tank has a 5 meter radius and is 21 meters in height: 3.14 × 21 × 5^2 = 3.14 × 21 × 25 = 1648.50 cubic meters

70) The correct answer is C. Step 1 – Calculate the volume of the large cone. The large cones are 6 inches high and have a 1.5 inch radius. The volume of a cone ≈ (3.14 × height × radius^2) ÷ 3 = (3.14 × 6 × 1.5 × 1.5) ÷ 3 = 14.13. Step 2 – Calculate the volume of the medium cone. The medium cones are 5 inches high and have a 1 inch radius: (3.14 × height × radius^2) ÷ 3 = (3.14 × 5 × 1 × 1) ÷ 3 = 5.23. Step 3 – Calculate the difference between the volume of the two cones: 14.13 – 5.23 = 8.90

71) The correct answer is C. Cobb County is the darkest bar, so it is the first bar for each month. It starts on 2.9, then goes down to 2.1, then 1.2, and finally 0.8. So, it decreases each month.

72) The correct answer is B. In June, Dawson County had 1.1 inches of rain and Emery County had 1.7 inches. Therefore, Emery County had 0.6 more inches of rainfall than Dawson County.

73) The correct answer is A. Emery County had the following amounts of rainfall: May = 2.5 inches; June = 1.8 inches; July = 1 inch; August = 0.9 inch. Then add these amounts together to solve: 2.5 + 1.8 + 1 + 0.9 = 6.2 inches in total

74) The correct answer is A. We already know that Emery County had 6.2 total inches of rainfall for the four months from our previous answer. So, add up the four months for Cobb County and then do the same for Dawson County. Cobb County: May = 2.9 inches; June = 2.1 inches; July = 1.2 inches; August 0.8 inches = 7 total inches. Dawson County: May = 3.5 inches; June = 1.1 inches; July = 0.9 inches; August = 2.3 inches = 7.8 total inches. Therefore, Emery County had the lowest total with 6.2 inches.

75) The correct answer is D. Reptiles account for 42% of the zoo creatures at the start of the year, and there are 1,500 creatures in total, so multiply to solve: 1,500 × 0.42 = 630 reptiles

76) The correct answer is B. At the end of last year, the 15% of the customers questioned expressed a preference for fish. This had increased to 16% at the end of this year.

77) The correct answer is C. Place the values for the temperatures in ascending order:
−10, −9, 1, 6, 8, 12, 13. The median is the one in the middle: −10, −9, 1 , **6** , 8, 12, 13

78) The correct answer is B. Add up all of the values: −10 + −9 + 1 + 6 + 8 + 12 + 13 = 21. Then divide by 7 for the seven days represented: 21 ÷ 7 = 3

79) The correct answer is D. None of the values occurs more than once, so there is no mode.

80) The correct answer is D. The range is the high minus the low: 13 − (−10) = 23

ATI TEAS Practice Problems 81 to 150 – Solutions and Explanations

81) The correct answer is D. Subtract the negative numbers as shown: –92 – 120 = –212. Remember to express your result as a negative number.

82) The correct answer is D. The problem states that he earns a $350 commission on every set of kitchen cupboards, so he earned the referral fee 11 times this week. We need to multiply the amount of the commission by the number of sets of cupboards to solve: $350 × 11 = $3850

83) The correct answer is B. The problem is asking for the total for all four months, so we add the four amounts together: $2516 + $3482 + $4871 + $5267 = $16,136

84) The correct answer is C. Divide the total amount by the number of members to solve: $2,496 ÷ 52 = $48.

85) The correct answer is A. Take the amount of money the customer gives the cashier and subtract the amount of the purchase: $150.00 – $127.82 = $22.18

86) The correct answer is A. Add the investment profits and subtract the business losses: –$1205 + $532 + $875 – $1359 + $1436 – $982 = –$703

87) The correct answer is B. Divide and then express the result as a percentage. Step 1 – Treat the line in the fraction as the division symbol: 6/25 = 6 ÷ 25 = 0.24. Step 2 – To express the result from Step 1 as a percentage, move the decimal point two places to the right and add the percent sign: 0.24 = 24%

88) The correct answer is C. If you are unsure, perform division on the answer choices to check: $^4/_5$ = 4 ÷ 5 = 0.8 = 80%

89) The correct answer is C. To express a decimal number as a percent, move the decimal point two places to the right and add the percent sign: 0.32 = 32.0%

90) The correct answer is B. Divide by 100 to express a percentage as a decimal. So, move the decimal point two places to the left and remove the percent sign: 25% = 25 ÷ 100 = 0.25

91) The correct answer is B. Multiply the total number of items by the decimal number given in the problem to solve: 50 items × 0.24 completed = 50 × 0.24 = 12 items

92) The correct answer is C. Perform division on the answer choices to check your answer: 1/5 = 1 ÷ 5 = 0.20

93) The correct answer is C. Multiply to solve: 15$^1/_2$ ounces × 20 cents per ounce = 15.50 × 0.20 = $3.10

94) The correct answer is C. Step 1 – Determine the amount of time worked in minutes: 35 hours × 60 minutes per hour = 2100 minutes. Step 2 – Divide by the amount of order forms to find the rate: 2100 minutes ÷ 210 order forms = 10 minutes each

81

95) The correct answer is D. Step 1 – Take the total number of families and divide this by 10, which is the number of families in the original ratio: 4500 ÷ 10 = 450. Step 2 – Take the result from Step 1 and multiply by the amount in the subset to solve: 450 × 7 = 3,150

96) The correct answer is A. Add to solve: −$1,503 + $2,476 − $3,087 + $986 = −$1,128

97) The correct answer is B. Step 1 – Add the gift wrap to the original price: $12 − $1.50 = $13.50. Step 2 – Take the result from Step 1 and multiply by the number of gifts sold: $13.50 × 51 = $688.50

98) The correct answer is C. Step 1 – Determine the total number of hours worked: 7 hours per day for 6 days = 7 × 6 = 42 hours. Step 2 – Calculate the profit the company makes per hour. The customer was billed $30 per hour for the employee's work, and the employee was paid $18 per hour: $30 − $18 = $12 profit per hour. Step 3 – Multiply the total hours by the profit per hour to solve: 42 hours × $12 profit per hour = $504

99) The correct answer is D. Take the amount of satisfactory responses and divide by the amount of total customers: 132 ÷ 150 = 0.88 = 88.0%

100) The correct answer is A. To find the average, calculate the total, and then divide by the number of days. Step 1 – Find the total: 106 + 110 + 108 + 112 + 104 = 540. Step 2 – Divide the result from Step 1 by the number of days: 540 ÷ 5 = 108

101) The correct answer is D. Step 1 – Add the whole numbers: 5 + 3 = 8. Step 2 – Add the fractions: 5/8 + 3/8 = 8/8. Step 3 – Simplify the fraction from Step 2: 8/8 = 1. Step 4 – Combine the results from Step 1 and Step 3 to solve the problem: 8 + 1 = 9

102) The correct answer is A. Step 1 – Subtract the whole numbers: 10 − 9 = 1. Step 2 – Subtract the fractions: 7/12 − 5/12 = 2/12. Step 3 – Simplify the fraction from Step 2: 2/12 = 1/6. Step 4 – Combine the results from Step 1 and Step 3 to get your new mixed number to solve the problem: 1 + 1/6 = $1^1/_6$. The amount after re-measuring was greater than the initial measurement, so $1^1/_6$ yards more fabric is needed.

103) The correct answer is C. Step 1 – Add the whole numbers: 25 + 32 = 57. Step 2 – Add the fractions: 7/16 + 2/16 = 9/16. Step 3 – Combine the results from Step 1 and Step 2 to get your new mixed number to solve the problem: 57 + 9/16 = $57^9/_{16}$

104) The correct answer is B. Step 1 – Take the 84 ounces for the mixture and divide by the 2 ounces of herbicide stated in the original ratio: 84 ÷ 2 = 42. Step 2 – Multiply the result from Step 1 by the 5 ounces of water stated in the original ratio to get your answer: 5 × 42 = 210

105) The correct answer is A. Step 1 – Take the total amount of mid-level managers stated in the problem and divide this by the 3 stated in the original ratio: 87 ÷ 3 = 29. Step 2 – Take the amount from Step 1 and multiply by the 2 upper-level managers from the original ratio to solve the problem: 29 × 2 = 58

106) The correct answer is D. Step 1 – Calculate the amount of time spent on the initial job: 9:15 to 9:35 = 20 minutes. Step 2 – Calculate the rate for 1 card: 20 minutes ÷ 2 cards made = 10 minutes per card. Step 3 – Determine how many minutes there are in 8 hours: 8 hours × 60 minutes = 480 minutes

available. Step 4 – Divide the total minutes by the rate per card to solve: 480 total minutes ÷ 10 minutes per card = 48 cards

107) The correct answer is B. Add the three figures together to solve: 75.25 + 10.75 + 3.20 = 89.2

108) The correct answer is A. Add the percentages together to solve: 45% + 35% = 80%

109) The correct answer is D. Step 1 – Convert the mixed number to a decimal: $2^1/_2$ = 2.5 hours.
Step 2 – Multiply this result by the number of units: 2.5 hours per unit × 5 units = 12.5 hours.
Step 3 – Convert the decimal to minutes: 0.5 hour = 30 minutes. Step 4 – Express your answer in hours and minutes: 12 hours and 30 minutes

110) The correct answer is D. We know that we have to round to the nearest hundredth. The hundredth decimal place is the number 2 positions to the right of the decimal. For example, 0.01 is 1 one hundredth.
In our question, the first jump of 3.246 is rounded up to 3.25
The second jump of 3.331 is rounded down to 3.33
The third jump of 3.328 is rounded up to 3.33
Then add these three figures together to get your answer: 3.25 + 3.33 + 3.33 = 9.91

111) The correct answer is D. Step 1 – Calculate the total amount of miles for the white lines for six years. There is a double white line, so we have to multiply by 2: 500 × 2 = 1,000 miles. Step 2 – Add in the amount for the yellow line = 1,000 + 200 = 1,200 miles total for six years. Step 3 – Double the result from the previous step to get the amount for 12 years: 1,200 × 2 = 2,400

112) The correct answer is A. For problems with decimals, line the figures up in a column and add zeroes to fill in the column as shown below:

A) 0.5400
B) 0.0540
C) 0.0450
D) 0.5045

If you still struggle with decimals, you can remove the decimal points and the zeroes before the other integers in order to see the answer more clearly.
A) 0̶.̶5400
B) 0̶.̶0̶540
C) 0̶.̶0̶450
D) 0̶.̶5045

When we have removed the zeroes in front of the other numbers, we can see that the largest number is the first one, which is 0.54.

113) The correct answer is A. Step 1 – Convert the first fraction to the common denominator: 5/8 = (5 × 2)/(8 × 2) = 10/16. Step 2 – Subtract one increment from this to get your result: 10/16 – 1/16 = 9/16

114) The correct answer is D. Step 1 – Determine the excess amount over the amount in the deal.

15 pairs needed – 12 pairs in the deal = 3 individual pairs remaining. Step 2 – Take the result from the previous step and multiply by the individual price: 3 × $1.50 = $4.50. Step 3 – Add the result from the previous step to the price for the 12 pairs in the deal to solve: $10 + 4.50 = $14.50

115) The correct answer is C. Add up the units that have passed inspection: 968 + 817 + 942 + 1018 + 879 = 4624. Then divide this by the number of days: 4624 ÷ 5 = 924.8, which we round to 925.

116) The correct answer is B. Step 1 – Work out the cost for the usual supplier: 120 units × $172 = $20,640. Step 2 – Calculate the price for the third supplier: $19,000 + ($19,000 × .07) = $19,000 + $1,330 = $20,330. Step 3 – Compare to other deals to solve. The other deals are $20,640 and $20,500, so $20,330 is the best deal.

117) The correct answer is A. Step 1 – Determine the dollar value of the markup on the first bag: $12 retail price – $4 cost = $8 markup. Step 2 – Calculate the percentage of the markup on the first bag by dividing the dollar value of the markup by the cost: $8 ÷ $4 = 2.00 = 200%. Step 3 – Use the percentage markup from the previous step to determine the dollar value of the markup on the second style of bag: $3 × 200% = $3 × 2 = $6. Step 4 – Add the dollar value of the markup for the second style of bag to the cost of the bag to get the retail price: $3 + $6 = $9

118) The correct answer is D. Step 1 – Determine the dollar value of the discount: $22.50 – $20 = $2.5. Step 2 – Divide the result from Step 1 by the original price to get the percentage: $2.50 ÷ $22.50 = 0.1111 = 11.11%, which we round to 11%.

119) The correct answer is A. To find the average, add up all of the items in the set and then divide by the amount of items in the set. (9.8 + 8.7 + 9.5 + 7.9 + 8.6 + 6.3 + 9.9 + 5.4) ÷ 8 = 66.1 ÷ 8 = 8.2625

120) The correct answer is A. The problem tells us that A is 3 times B, and B is 3 more than 6 times C. So, we need to create equations based on this information.
B is 3 more than 6 times C: B = 6C + 3
A is 3 times B: A = 3B
Since B = 6C + 3, we can substitute 6C + 3 for B in the second equation as follows:
A = 3B
A = 3(6C + 3)
A = 18C + 9
So, A is 9 more than 18 times C.

121) The correct answer is B. For problems this like, use the following steps. Step 1 – Express the percentage tax rate as a decimal: 8.5% = 0.085. Step 2 – Add 1 to the result from Step 1. The value of 1 represents the price of the item before tax: 1 + 0.085 = 1.085. Step 3 – Divide the price after tax by the result from Step 2 to get the price before tax: $217 ÷ 1.085 = $200

122) The correct answer is D. To calculate a reverse percentage you need to divide, rather than multiply. So, take the $123 discount and divide by the 40% percentage: $123 ÷ 40% = $123 ÷ 0.40 = $307.50

123) The correct answer is D. Step 1 – Determine the rate for the manicures: 5 hours ÷ 4 manicures = 1.25 hours per manicure = 1 hour and 15 minutes per manicure. Step 2 – Calculate the time needed for all 20 manicures: 1.25 hours per manicure × 20 manicures = 25 hours. Step 3 – Determine the rate for

the pedicures: 2.5 hours ÷ 5 pedicures = 0.5 hours per pedicure. Step 4 – Calculate the time needed to do all 25 pedicures: 0.5 hours × 25 pedicures = 12.5 hours = 12 hours and 30 minutes. Step 5 – Find the total for all of the manicures and pedicures: 25 hours + 12.5 hours = 37.5 hours = 37 hours and 30 minutes

124) The correct answer is C. Step 1 – Calculate the daily rate in terms of a daily percentage: 57.75% ÷ 7 days = 8.25% per day. Step 2 – Divide this amount into 100% to find the approximate number of days in total: 100% ÷ 8.25% per day = 12.12 days, which we round down to 12 days.

125) The correct answer is C. Step 1 – Determine the cost for the first supplier: 135 units × $15.30 per unit = $2,065.50. The tax on this is: $2,065.50 × 0.06 = $123.93, so the total cost is: $2,065.50 + $123.93 = $2189.43. Step 2 – The total cost for the other supplier is: $2,100 + 75 = $2,175. So, you will get the best price from the second company.

126) The correct answer is D. Step 1 – Add the whole numbers: 4 + 3 = 7. Step 2 – Add the fractions: 3/8 + 7/8 = 10/8. Step 3 – Simplify the fraction from Step 2: 10/8 = 8/8 + 2/8 = 1 + 2/8 = $1^2/_8$ = $1^1/_4$.
Step 4 – Combine the results from Step 1 and Step 3 to solve the problem: 7 + $1^1/_4$ = $8^1/_4$

127) The correct answer is B. $7x$ is between 5 and 6, so set up an inequality as follows:
$5 < 7x < 6$
Then insert the fractions from the answer choices for the value of x to solve the problem.
$5 < \left(7 \times {}^3/_4\right) < 6$
$5 < [(7 \times 3) \div 4] < 6$
$5 < (21 \div 4) < 6$
$5 < 5.25 < 6$
5.25 is between 5 and 6, so ${}^3/_4$ is the correct answer.

128) The correct answer is C. To calculate the range, the low number in the set is deducted from the high number in the set. The problem set is: 98.5, 85.5, 80.0, 97, 93, 92.5, 93, 87, 88, 82.
The high number is 98.5 and the low number is 80, so the range is 18.5 (98.5 – 80 = 18.5)

129) The correct answer is A. Step 1 – Add the cups: 2 cups + 3 cups = 5 cups. Step 2 – Convert the result from Step 1 to quarts and cups. There are 4 cups in one quart: 5 cups = 1 quart and 1 cup.
Step 3 – Add the result from the previous step to the number of full quarts stated in the question: 3 quarts + 4 quarts + 1 quart and 1 cup = 8 quarts and 1 cup. Step 4 – Convert to gallons if possible. There are 4 quarts in one gallon: 8 quarts and 1 cup = 2 gallons and 1 cup

130) The correct answer is B. From the formula, we can see that 1 mile = 1.61 kilometers. So, multiply to solve: 38 miles × 1.61 = 61.18 kilometers, which we round to 61.

131) The correct answer is A. Step 1 – Find the total weight of the product by subtracting the weight of the empty crate. The crate weighs 90 pounds and 12 ounces when it contains the product and 15 pounds when it is empty, so the product itself weighs: 90 pounds and 12 ounces – 15 pounds = 75 pounds and 12 ounces. Step 2 – Use the formula to convert the total weight of the product from pounds and ounces to just ounces. 1 pound = 16 ounces, so 75 pounds and 12 ounces = (75 × 16) + 12 = 1200 + 12 = 1212 ounces. Step 3 – The problem tells us that each can of tomato sauce weighs 12 ounces. Take the total

weight from the previous step and divide by the weight per unit to determine how many units the crate contains: 1212 ounces ÷ 12 ounces per unit = 101 units

132) The correct answer is B. 1 foot = 0.3048 meters, so to convert to meters we need to multiply feet by 0.3048. 1 meter = 1,000 millimeters, so to convert from meters to millimeters, we need to multiply again by 1,000. So, the correct formula is as follows: millimeters = feet × 0.3048 × 1,000

133) The correct answer is B. Step 1 – Calculate the mean high temperature in Fahrenheit. To do so, find the total for all five days and divide the result by 5: (72 + 68 + 65 + 82 + 81) ÷ 5 = 368 ÷ 5 = 73.6°F average. Step 2 – Convert the mean in Fahrenheit to Celsius using the formula from the formula sheet. To convert Fahrenheit to Celsius, we use this formula: °C = 0.56(°F – 32) = 0.56(73.6° – 32) = 0.56(41.6) = 0.56 × 41.6 = 23.296, which we round to 23°C.

134) The correct answer is A. From the formula, we know that the area of a rectangle = length × width. Here, we are given the area, so we need to divide that by the length in order to get the width: 360 ÷ 30 = 12 feet

135) The correct answer is D. Step 1 – Calculate the dimensions of the floor in inches: 8 feet × 12 inches per foot = 96 inches long; 4 feet × 12 inches in a foot = 48 inches wide. Step 2 – Determine how many wooden pieces will fit along the length of the floor. If we lay the 12-inch side of the wooden piece against the length of the room, we can lay 8 of these side by side to cover the 96-inch length: 96 ÷ 12 = 8. Step 3 – Determine how many wooden pieces can fit along the width. 48-inch-wide floor ÷ 6-inch-wide pieces = 48 ÷ 6 = 8 pieces. Step 4 – Multiply the results from steps 2 and 3 to get the total number of pieces needed for the job: 8 × 8 = 64

136) The correct answer is C. area of a rectangle = length × width. The wall is 16 feet by 11 feet, so multiply to solve: 16 × 11 = 176

137) The correct answer is A. We know that the volume of a rectangular solid = length × width × height. Here, we are given the volume, so we need to divide that by the length and then the width in order to find the height: (1080 ÷ 12) ÷ 9 = 90 ÷ 9 = 10 feet

138) The correct answer is B. Step 1 – Find the volume in terms of cubic inches. Remember that radius is half of diameter. Here we have a diameter of 12, so the radius is 6. Cylinder volume ≈ 3.14 × radius^2 × height ≈ 3.14 × 6^2 × 18 ≈ 3.14 × 36 × 18 ≈ 2034.72. Step 2 – Convert the volume in cubic inches to gallons. 1 gallon = 231 cubic inches, so divide by 231 to convert to gallons: 2034.72 ÷ 231 = 8.8 gallons

139) The correct answer is D. Step 1 – First we need to calculate the volume in terms of cubic feet. The volume of a cube = (length of side)^3. The length of the side is 9 feet, so the volume is 9 × 9 × 9 = 729 cubic feet. Step 2 – We have to convert the result from Step 1 to cubic inches. From the formula, we can see that 1 cubic foot = 1,728 cubic inches, so multiply to solve: 729 × 1,728 = 1,259,712 cubic inches

140) The correct answer is D. Step 1 – Calculate the volume of the container when it is full. The container is 25 feet long, 12 feet wide and 18 feet high. To find the volume of a rectangular solid, we use the formula: length × width × height = 25 × 12 × 18 = 5,400 cubic feet. Step 2 – Calculate how much product is in the container. The container is now 75% full: 5,400 cubic feet × 0.75 = 4,050 cubic feet

141) The correct answer is C. Step 1 – Calculate the amount of remaining stock in quarts and ounces: [2 × (16 cups and 7 ounces)] + [3 × (20 cups and 4 ounces)] = 32 cups and 14 ounces + 60 cups and 12 ounces = 92 cups and 26 ounces. Step 2 – Convert the existing stock from cups to quarts: 1 quart = 4 cups, so divide the amount of cups by 4 to convert to quarts: (92 cups ÷ 4) + 26 ounces = 23 quarts and 26 ounces. There are 32 ounces in a quart, so we cannot convert the remaining 26 ounces to quarts. Step 3 – Calculate the amount required to restock. 50 quarts are required in total, and you have approximately 23 quarts on hand, so subtract to find out how many more quarts you need to get the stock back up to 50 quarts: 50 − 23 = 27 quarts needed. Step 4 – The chemical comes in 5-quart containers, so calculate how many containers you need to buy to cover the 27 quarts that are required: 27 ÷ 5 = 5.4 quarts. It is not possible to buy a fractional part of a container, so you have to buy 6 containers.

142) The correct answer is D. Step 1 – Calculate the volume of each vat: length × width × height = 10 × 10 × 12 = 1,200 cubic feet. Step 2 – Determine how full each vat is in terms of cubic feet. Vat 1: 1,200 × $^3/_4$ = 1,200 × 0.75 = 900 cubic feet. Vat 2: 1,200 × $^4/_5$ = 1,200 × 0.80 = 960 cubic feet. Step 3 – Add the volume of the two vats together to determine the total volume: 900 + 960 = 1,860 cubic feet. Step 4 – Convert the cubic feet to cubic inches. 1 cubic foot = 1,728 cubic inches, so we multiply to convert: 1,860 cubic feet × 1,728 = 3,214,080 cubic inches. Step 5 – Multiply by the price to solve: 3,214,080 cubic inches × $0.12 = $385,689.60, which we round to $385,690.

143) The correct answer is B. Step 1 – Calculate the radius of the cone. The diameter is 6 and radius is half of diameter, so the radius is 3. Step 2 – Calculate the volume of the cone. The formula for the volume of a cone ≈ (3.14 × radius^2 × height) ÷ 3 = (3.14 × 3^2 × 8) ÷ 3 = 226.08 ÷ 3 = 75.36 cubic feet.

144) The correct answer is B. No lights are to be installed in the corners, so each of the two 10-feet walls will have 1 light installed in the middle of each wall: 10 ÷ 5 = 2, but we subtract 1 from this for the corner. So, we have 1 light on each of the 2 shorter walls, which accounts for 2 lights so far. Each of the 25-foot walls have 5 increments of 5 feet, and again no lights are in the corners: (25 ÷ 5) − 1 = 4. So, each of the 2 long walls will have 4 lights on each wall. So there will be 10 lights in total on the walls in the room (1 + 1 + 4 + 4 = 10). You may wish to draw a diagram on your scratch paper when solving problems like this one.

145) The correct answer is D. Step 1 – Calculate the volume of the large ice cube: (1.8 × 1.8 × 1.8) = 5.832. Step 2 – Calculate the volume of the small ice cube: (1.4 × 1.4 × 1.4) = 2.744. Step 3 – Calculate the difference between the volume of the two ice cubes: 5.832 − 2.744 = 3.088

146) The correct answer is D. Step 1 – Calculate the area of the large triangle: (12 × 18) ÷ 2 = 216 ÷ 2 = 108. Step 2 – Calculate the area of the small triangle: (8 × 14) ÷ 2 = 112 ÷ 2 = 56. Step 3 – Subtract to solve: 108 − 56 = 52

147) The correct answer is D. The total number of patients is 793,000 and 89% of them have survived, so multiply to solve: 793,000 × 0.89 = 705,770

148) The correct answer is. C. This is a more complicated question. You need to determine the death rate, so subtract the survival rate from 100% to get the death rate for each category. Then multiply for each category and compare:
Cardiopulmonary and vascular deaths: 602,000 × 0.18 = 108,360
HIV/AIDS deaths: 215,000 × 0.27 = 58,050

Diabetes deaths: 793,000 × 0.11 = 87,230
Cancer and leukemia deaths: 231,000 × 0.52 =120,120
Deaths from premature birth complications: 68,000 × 0.36 = 24,480
So cancer and leukemia caused the greatest number of deaths.

149) The correct answer is C. Cancer and leukemia deaths: 231,000 × 0.52 = 120,120, which is closest to 120,000.

150) The correct answer is D. Diabetes patients have a survival rate of 89%, which is the highest survival rate of any patient group in the data set.

ATI TEAS Practice Test 1 – Solutions and Explanations

151) The correct answer is C. The problem states that you get a $59 subscription for every new customer, so we need to multiply the amount of the subscription fee by the number of new customers to solve: $59 × 14 = $826

152) The correct answer is D. Perform the operation as shown: 35 – (–92) = 127. Express your result as a positive number since the value has increased from year 1 to year 2.

153) The correct answer is D. Set up your equation to calculate the average, using x for the age of the 5th sibling:
$(2 + 5 + 7 + 12 + x) ÷ 5 = 8$
$(2 + 5 + 7 + 12 + x) ÷ 5 × 5 = 8 × 5$
$(2 + 5 + 7 + 12 + x) = 40$
$26 + x = 40$
$26 – 26 + x = 40 – 26$
$x = 14$

154) The correct answer is A. Subtract to solve: 75.00 – 8.35 = 66.65

155) The correct answer is B. The problem provides the number set: 8.19, 7.59, 8.25, 7.35, 9.10
First of all, put the numbers in ascending order: 7.35, 7.59, 8.19, 8.25, 9.10
Then find the one that is in the middle: 7.35, 7.59, **8.19**, 8.25, 9.10

156) The correct answer is C. Step 1 – Determine the total number of hours worked: 7.5 hours per day for 2 days = 7.5 × 2 = 15 hours. Step 2 – Calculate the profit your company makes per hour. The customer was billed $75 per hour for your work, and you were paid $40 per hour: $75 – $40 = $35 profit per hour. Step 3 – Multiply the total number of hours by the profit per hour to solve: 15 hours × $35 profit per hour = $525

157) The correct answer is C. The value of μ must be greater than $^{11}/_3$, which is equal to 3.6667. The answer 4.1 is the only option which meets this criterion.

158) The correct answer is C. In this problem, the fraction on the second number is larger than the fraction on the first number, so we need to covert the first fraction before we start our calculation. Step 1 – Convert $12^7/_{16}$ for subtraction: $12^7/_{16} = 11^7/_{16} + 1 = 11^7/_{16} + {}^{16}/_{16} = 11^{23}/_{16}$. Step 2 – There were $8^9/_{16}$ yards left, so subtract the whole numbers: 11 – 8 = 3. Step 3 – Subtract the fractions: 23/16 – 9/16 = 14/16. Step 4 – Simplify the fraction from Step 3: 14/16 = (14 ÷ 2)/(16 ÷ 2) = 7/8. Step 4 – Combine the results from Step 2 and Step 4 to get your new mixed number to solve the problem: $3 + 7/8 = 3^7/_8$

159) The correct answer is B. The problem tells us the relative amount of units sold, but the question is asking for the relative amount of units left. So, subtract the decimal from 1 to find the relative amount left: 1 – 0.75 = 0.25. Then multiply the total number of items at the start by this decimal number: 80 items × 0.25 = 80 × 0.25 = 20 items left

160) The correct answer is C. Step 1 – Set up the original proportion as a fraction. We have 3 parts of icing sugar for every 6 parts of sugar paste so our fraction is $^3/_6$. Step 2 – You can simplify the fraction

from the previous step because both the numerator and denominator are divisible by 3: $^3/_6 \div ^3/_3 = ^1/_2.$ Step 3 – We need to use 14 parts of sugar paste for the current batch, so multiply this amount by the simplified fraction. $^1/_2 \times 14 = 7$

161) The correct answer is A. This problem is asking for the ratio of non-faulty mp3 players to the quantity of faulty mp3 players. Therefore, you must put the quantity of non-faulty mp3 players before the colon in the ratio. In this problem, 1% of the players are faulty. 1% × 100 = 1 faulty player in every 100 players. 100 − 1 = 99 non-faulty players. So, the ratio is 99:1. The number before the colon and the number after the colon can be added together to get the total quantity.

162) The correct answer is B. The sales price of each cell phone is four times the cost. The cost is expressed as x, so the sales price is $4x$. The difference between the sales price of each cell phone and the cost of each cell phone is the profit. In this problem, the sales price is $4x$ and the cost is x.
Sales Price − Cost = Profit
$4x − x$ = Profit
$3x$ = Profit

163) The correct answer is B. Step 1 – Subtract one increment: 23/64 − 1/64 = 22/64. Step 2 – Simplify your result: 22/64 = (22 ÷ 2)/(64 ÷ 2) = 11/32

164) The correct answer is B. Step 1 – Work out the cost for the usual supplier: 325 pairs × $4 = $1,300. Step 2 – Calculate the price for the second supplier: $1,250 + ($1,250 × .06) = $1,250 + $75 = $1,325. Step 3 – Compare to the third deal to solve: The third deal is $1,290 so this is the best deal.

165) The correct answer is B. Take the total cost after tax and divide by 1 plus the tax rate to get the cost before tax: $344.50 ÷ 1.06 = $325

166) The correct answer is C. The left hand side of the inequality will always be negative since there is a minus sign in front of the absolute value symbol. The right hand side of the inequality will always be positive since the operation is performed inside the absolute value symbol. So, the left hand side of the inequality will always be less than the right hand side of the inequality. Therefore, any positive or negative real number will satisfy the inequality.

167) The correct answer is C. The second number after the decimal, which is the number 7, is in the hundredths place. This is followed by a number less than five, so we round down to 95,324.8700.

168) The correct answer is D. We have the following numbers in our problem:
0.0012
0.0253
0.2135
0.3152

If you still do not feel confident with decimals, remember that you can remove the decimal point and the zeroes after the decimal but before the other integers in order to see the answer more clearly.

    12
   253
  2135
  3152

169) The correct answer is D. Ten out of 25 students participate in drama club. First of all, express the relationship as a fraction: $^{10}/_{25}$

Then divide to find the percentage: $^{10}/_{25} = 10 \div 25 = 0.40 = 40\%$

Finally, choose the pie chart that has 40% of its area shaded in dark gray.

170) The correct answer is D. The most striking relationship on the graph is the line for ages 65 and over, which clearly shows a negative relationship between exercising outdoors and the number of days of rain per month. You will recall that a negative relationship exists when an increase in one variable causes a decrease in the other variable. So, we can conclude that people aged 65 and over seem less inclined to exercise outdoors when there is more rain.

171) The correct answer is C. We have a formula to convert meters to centimeters and another formula to convert inches to centimeters, so we will need to use those two formulas to solve the problem.
Step 1 – Determine the measurement in centimeters: 1 meter = 100 centimeters. Step 2 – Convert the centimeters to inches. The formulas states that 1 inch = 2.54 centimeters. However, we need to use the formula in reverse because we are converting centimeters to inches. So, divide to solve: 100 ÷ 2.54 = 39.37 inches

172) The correct answer is C. The sum of all three angles inside a triangle is always 180 degrees. So, we need to deduct the degrees given from 180° to find out the total degrees of the two other angles:
180° − 36° = 144°. Now divide this result by two in order to determine the degrees for each angle:
144° ÷ 2 = 72°

173) The correct answer is A. The area of a rectangle is equal to its length times its width. This football field is 30 yards wide and 100 yards long, so we can substitute the values into the appropriate formula.
rectangle area = width × length
rectangle area = 30 × 100
rectangle area = 3000

174)   The correct answer is B. You are being asked about the distance around the outside, so you need to calculate the perimeter, Write out the formula: (length × 2) + (width × 2). Then substitute the values:
(5 × 2) + (3 × 2) = 10 + 6 = 16

175) The correct answer is B. Substitute the value of the diameter into the formula to solve.
circumference ≈ diameter × 3.14
circumference ≈ 12 × 3.14

176) The correct answer is D. To calculate the volume of a box, you need the formula for a rectangular solid: volume = base × width × height. Now substitute the values from the problem into the formula. volume = 20 × 15 × 25 = 7500

177) The correct answer is D. We have the data set: 1.6, 2.9, 4.5, 2.5, 2.5, 5.1, and 5.4. The mode is the number that occurs most frequently. 2.5 occurs twice, but the other numbers only occur once. So, 2.5 is the mode.

178) The correct answer is B. Step 1 – Find the total product weight, excluding the weight of the crate. 447 pounds – 60 pounds = 387 pounds. Step 2 – Convert the total product weight to ounces. 387 pounds × 16 ounces per pound = 6,192 ounces of total product weight. Step 3 – Covert the weight of each unit to ounces: 32 pounds and 4 ounces = (32 × 16) + 4 = 512 + 4 = 516 ounces each. Step 4 – Divide to solve: 6,192 ÷ 516 = 12 units

179) The correct answer is C. Step 1 – Determine the actual distance between the two cities in miles. 1 inch on the map = 20 miles, so 2.5 inches × 20 = 50 miles actual distance. Step 2 – Convert the result from Step 1 to kilometers. 1 mile = 1.61 kilometers, so 50 miles × 1.61 = 80.5 kilometers.

180) The correct answer is A. The total amount of the budget is $65,000. The up-front cost is $7,500, so we can determine the remaining amount of available funds by deducting the up-front cost from the total: $65,000 – $7,500. We have to divide the available amount by the number of employees (E) to get the maximum cost per employee: ($65,000 – $7,500) ÷ E

181) The correct answer is A.

Perform the multiplication on the terms in the parentheses.
$2(3x − 1) = 4(x + 1) − 3$
$6x − 2 = (4x + 4) − 3$

Then simplify.
$6x − 2 = (4x + 4) − 3$
$6x − 2 = 4x + 1$
$6x − 2 − 1 = 4x + 1 − 1$
$6x − 3 = 4x$

Then isolate x to get your answer.
$6x − 3 = 4x$
$6x − 4x − 3 = 4x − 4x$
$2x − 3 = 0$
$2x − 3 + 3 = 0 + 3$
$2x = 3$
$2x ÷ 2 = 3 ÷ 2$
$x = {}^3/_2$

182) The correct answer is B. 70 square feet × $5.50 per piece = $385 total cost

183) The correct answer is C. Subtract the percentage of the discount from 100% to get the percentage of the price to be paid: 100% - 27.5% = 72.5%. Multiply to solve: $385 × 72.5% = $279.13, which is closest to $280.

184) The correct answer is D. To answer this type of question, you need these principles: Positive numbers are greater than negative numbers; (b) When two fractions have the same numerator, the fraction with the smaller number in the denominator is the larger fraction. Accordingly, 1 is greater than $\frac{1}{5}$; $\frac{1}{5}$ is greater than $\frac{1}{7}$, and $\frac{1}{7}$ is greater than $-\frac{1}{3}$.

185) The correct answer is C. Add 9 to each side to get rid of the integer on the left.
$3x - 9 = -18$
$3x - 9 + 9 = -18 + 9$
$3x = -9$
Then divide each side by 3 to solve.
$3x \div 3 = -9 \div 3$
$x = -3$

186) The correct answer is A. Substitute 7 for x to solve.
$2x^2 + 8x =$
$[2(7)^2] + (8 \times 7) =$
$(2 \times 49) + 56 =$
$98 + 56 = 154$

ATI TEAS Practice Test 2 – Solutions and Explanations

187) The correct answer is B. Divide the total amount by the sales price per unit to solve: $7,375 ÷ $59 = 125 units sold

188) The correct answer is D. Place the integers on one side of the inequality.
$-3x + 14 < 5$
$-3x + 14 - 14 < 5 - 14$
$-3x < -9$

Then get rid of the negative number. We need to reverse the way that the inequality sign points because we are dividing by a negative.
$-3x < -9$
$-3x ÷ -3 > -9 ÷ -3$ ("Less than" becomes "greater than" because we divide by a negative number.)
$x > 3$
4.35 is greater than 3, so it is the correct answer.

189) The correct answer is C. Divide and then express the result as a percentage. Step 1 – Treat the line in the fraction as the division symbol: 6/25 = 6 ÷ 25 = 0.24. Step 2 – To express the result from Step 1 as a percentage, move the decimal point two places to the right and add the percent sign: 0.24 = 24.0%

190) The correct answer is C. Move the decimal point two places to the right and add the percent sign: 0.40 = 40.0%

191) The correct answer is D. First of all, you need to determine the difference in temperature during the entire time period: 62 – 38 = 24 degrees less. Then calculate how much time has passed. From 5:00 PM to 11:00 PM, 6 hours have passed. Next, divide the temperature difference by the amount of time that has passed to get the temperature change per hour: 24 degrees ÷ 6 hours = 4 degrees less per hour. To calculate the temperature at the stated time, you need to calculate the time difference. From 5:00 PM to 9:00 PM, 4 hours have passed. So, the temperature difference during the stated time is 4 hours × 4 degrees per hour = 16 degrees less. Finally, deduct this from the beginning temperature to get your final answer: 62°F – 16°F = 46°F

192) The correct answer is C. If they bought 3 hamburgers they paid $12 for these since 3 × $4 = 12. Subtract this value from the total purchase of $22: $22 – $12 = $10. So they ate $10 worth of hot dogs. Hot dogs cost $2.%0 each, so divide to solve: $10.00 ÷ $2.50 = 4 hot dogs

193) The correct answer is A. Remember the two concepts: (a) Negative numbers are less than positive numbers; (b) When two fractions have the same numerator, the fraction with the smaller number in the denominator is the larger fraction. So, $-^1/_4$ is less than $^1/_8$, $^1/_8$ is less than $^1/_6$, and $^1/_6$ is less than 1.

194) The correct answer is B. The number is 10.005. The third number after the decimal, which is 0 in answer B, is in the thousandths place. The number after this is 5, so we round up to 10.001.

195) The correct answer is A. 53.1 is rounded down to 53; 9.912 is rounded up to 10; and 6.4 is rounded down to 6.

196) The correct answer is B. You need to find the lowest common denominator. Then add the numerators together as shown.

$$\frac{x}{5} + \frac{y}{2} =$$

$$\left(\frac{x}{5} \times \frac{2}{2}\right) + \left(\frac{y}{2} \times \frac{5}{5}\right) =$$

$$\frac{2x}{10} + \frac{5y}{10} =$$

$$\frac{2x + 5y}{10}$$

197) The correct answer is B. To solve this type of problem, do multiplication on the items in parentheses first.

$3x - 2(x + 5) = -8$
$3x - 2x - 10 = -8$

Then deal with the integers by putting them on one side of the equation.
$3x - 2x - 10 + 10 = -8 + 10$
$3x - 2x = 2$

Then solve for x.
$3x - 2x = 2$
$1x = 2$
$x = 2$

198) The correct answer is C. For your first step, determine how many square feet there are in total: 2000 square feet per room × 8 rooms = 16,000 square feet in total. Then you need to divide by the coverage rate: 16,000 square feet to cover ÷ 900 square feet coverage per bucket = 17.77 buckets needed. It is not possible to purchase a partial bucket of paint, so 17.77 is rounded up to 18 buckets of paint.

199) The correct answer is A. Divide the distance traveled by the time in order to get the speed in miles per hour. Remember that in order to divide by a fraction, you need to invert the fraction, and then multiply.
3.6 miles ÷ $^3/_4$ =
3.6 × $^4/_3$ =
(3.6 × 4) ÷ 3 =
14.4 ÷ 3 = 4.8 miles per hour

200) The correct answer is C. Step 1 – Determine the dollar amount of the reduction or discount: $60 original price – $45 sale price = $15 discount. Step 2 – Then divide the discount by the original price to get the percentage of the discount: $15 ÷ $60 = 0.25 = 25%

201) The correct answer is B. For your first step, add the subsets of the ratio together: 6 + 7 = 13. Then divide this into the total: 117 ÷ 13 = 9. Finally, multiply the result from the previous step by the subset of males from the original ratio: 6 × 9 = 54 males in the class

202) The correct answer is C. For 2 sandwiches, the total price is $17.50, so each sandwich in this deal sells for $8.75: $17.50 total price ÷ 2 sandwiches = $8.75 each. For 4 sandwiches, the total price is $34.40, so each sandwich in this deal sells for $8.60: $34.40 total price ÷ 4 sandwiches = $8.60 each. For 8 sandwiches, the total price is $68, so each sandwich in this deal sells for $8.50: $68 total price ÷ 8 sandwiches = $8.50 each. So, the best price per sandwich is $8.50.

203) The correct answer is B. First, determine the total sales value of the cheese and pepperoni pizzas based on the prices stated in the problem: (15 cheese pizzas × $10 each) + (10 pepperoni pizzas × $12 each) = $150 + $120 = $270. The remaining amount is allocable to the vegetable pizzas: Total sales of $310 − $270 = $40 worth of vegetable pizzas. The problems states that 5 vegetable pizzas were sold. We calculate the price of the vegetable pizzas as follows: $40 worth of vegetable pizzas ÷ 5 vegetable pizzas sold = $8 per vegetable pizza

204) The correct answer is C. Shanika wants to earn $4,000 this month. She gets the $1,000 basic pay regardless of the number of cars she sells, so we need to subtract that from the total first: $4,000 − $1,000 = $3,000. She gets $390 for each car she sells, so we need to divide that into the remaining $3,000: $3,000 to earn ÷ $390 per car = 7.69 cars to sell. Since it is not possible to sell a part of a car, we need to round up to 8 cars.

205) The correct answer is D. First, we can perform division to determine that the plane travels 6.5 miles per minute: 780 miles ÷ 120 minutes = 6.5 miles per minute. Since the plane travels at a constant speed, we multiply this amount by 40 minutes to solve: 6.5 miles per minute × 40 minutes = 260 miles

206) The correct answer is D. Step 1 – Determine the amount of time in seconds: 2 minutes and 48 seconds = (2 minutes × 60 seconds per minute) + 48 seconds = 120 seconds + 48 seconds = 168 seconds. Step 2 – Divide by the amount of furlongs to find the rate: 168 seconds ÷ 12 furlongs = 14 seconds per furlong

207) The correct answer is C. Step 1 – Take the total number of viewers and divide this by the 100 viewers in the original ratio: 3200 ÷ 100 = 32. Step 2 – Take the result from Step 1 and multiply by the amount in the subset to solve: 32 × 30 = 960

208) The correct answer is A. Step 1 – Add the charge for postage and handling to the original price per item: $22 + $ 3 = $25. Step 2 – Take the result from Step 1 and multiply by the number of items sold: $25 × 32 = $800

209) The correct answer is B. Step 1 – Add the whole numbers: 107 + 96 = 203. Step 2 – Add the fractions: 3/8 + 1/8 = 4/8 = 1/2. Step 3 – Combine the results from Step 1 and Step 2 to get your new mixed number to solve the problem: 203 + 1/2 = 203$^{1}/_{2}$

210) The correct answer is C. Add the four figures together to solve: 163.75 + 107.50 + 91.25 + 10.30 = 372.80

211) The correct answer is B. Step 1 – Find the amount of material needed for each quilt: 2 yards red, 4 yards blue, 1.2 yards gold (6 ÷ 5 = 1.2), and 0.5 yards white = 2 + 4 + 1.2 + 0.5 = 7.7 yards each. Step 2 – Multiply the total number of quilts by the amount of yards per quilt to solve: 10 × 7.7 = 77

212) The correct answer is A. The mode is the number that occurs the most frequently in the set. Our data set is: 1, 1, 3, 2, 4, 3, 1, 2, 1. The number 1 occurs 4 times in the set, which is more frequently than any other number in the set, so the mode is 1.

213) The correct answer is D. Calculate the length of strapping for the piece that goes over the front of the package: 22 + 42 + 22 + 42 = 128. Then calculate the length of strapping for the piece that goes over the top of the package: 20 + 42 + 20 + 42 = 124. Then add the 15 inches for the handle: 128 + 124 + 15 = 267 total inches

214) The correct answer is C. Each panel is 8 feet 6 inches long, and you need 11 panels to cover the entire side of the field. So, we need to multiply 8 feet 6 inches by 11. Step 1 – 8 feet × 11 = 88 feet. Step 2 – 6 inches × 11 = 66 inches. Step 3 – Now simplify the result. There are 12 inches in a foot, so we need to determine how many feet and inches there are in 66 inches. 66 inches ÷ 12 = 5 feet 6 inches. Step 4 – Add the two results together. 88 feet + 5 feet 6 inches = 93 feet 6 inches.

215) The correct answer is C. Since we are dealing with a square, all four sides of the floor are equal to each other. The tiles are also square, so they also have equal sides. Therefore, we can simply divide to get the answer: 64 ÷ 4 = 16

216) The correct answer is A. The volume of a cylinder is calculated as follows: volume ≈ 3.14 × $(radius)^2$ × *height* ≈ 3.14 × $(5)^2$ × 10 ≈ 785

217) The correct answer is A. First, we need to calculate the volume of cone A: (3.14 × 9^2 × 18) ÷ 3 = 1526.04. Then, we need to calculate the volume of Cone B: (3.14 × 3^2 × 6) ÷ 3 = 56.52. Then divide to get the ratio: 1526.04 ÷ 56.52 = 27. So, we can express the ratio as: $^{27}/_1$ = 27

218) The correct answer is A. Company B goes down in August, and Company C goes down in October. Company A, which is represented by the line with the diamonds, goes up every month from July to December.

219) The correct answer is B. Deal with the whole numbers first.

$6 + \frac{x}{4} \geq 22$

$6 - 6 + \frac{x}{4} \geq 22 - 6$

$\frac{x}{4} \geq 16$

Then eliminate the fraction.

$\frac{x}{4} \geq 16$

$4 \times \frac{x}{4} \geq 16 \times 4$

$x \geq 64$

220) The correct answer is C. The question is asking us how many residents have more than 3 relatives nearby, so we need to add the bars for 4 and 5 relatives from the chart. 20 residents have 4 relatives nearby and 10 residents have 5 relatives nearby, so 30 residents (20 + 10 = 30) have more than 3 relatives nearby.

221) The correct answer is B. First calculate how many correct answers there were: 12 + 20 + 32 + 32 = 96. Then calculate how many questions were on the test in total: 15 + 25 + 35 + 45 = 120. Finally, divide to solve 96 ÷ 120 = 0.80 = 80%

222) The correct answer is D. Take the total dollar amount and multiply by the 27% for education: $5,275,300 × 0.27 = $1,424,331

ATI TEAS Practice Test 3 – Solutions and Explanations

223) The correct answer is D. Covert the cups to quarter cups: 10 cups = 40 quarter cups. Then combine the whole number with the fraction and multiply to solve: $40^{1}/_{4}$ × 50 cents per quarter cup = 40.25 × 0.50 = $20.50

224) The correct answer is C. 1 yard = 36 inches, so we need to multiply by the number of yards: 6 yards × 36 inches = 216 inches

225) The correct answer is C. Step 1 – Take the total number of employees and divide this by 5: 250 ÷ 5 = 50. Step 2 – The question asks how many questionnaires have not been completed and returned, so subtract to find the amount in the 'not returned' subset: 5 – 4 = 1. Step 3 – Multiply the result from step 2 by the result from step 1 to solve: 50 × 1 = 50

226) The correct answer is D. Step 1 – Determine the total for sales in December: $20 × 55 = $1,100. Step 2 – Determine the total sales for January: $12 × 20 = $240. Step 3 – Add these two amounts to solve: $1,100 + $240 = $1,340

227) The correct answer is A. The problem tells us that the morning flight had 52 passengers more than the evening flight, and there were 540 passengers in total on the two flights that day. Step 1 – First of all, we need to deduct the difference from the total: 540 – 52 = 488. In other words, there were 488 passengers on both flights combined, plus the 52 additional passengers on the morning flight. Step 2 – Now divide this result by 2 to allocate an amount of passengers to each flight: 488 ÷ 2 = 244 passengers on the evening flight. (Had the question asked you for the amount of passengers on the morning flight, you would have had to add back the amount of additional passengers to find the total amount of passengers for the morning flight: 244 + 52 = 296 passengers on the morning flight)

228) The correct answer is D. You need to find the total points for all the females and the total points for all the males: Females: 60 × 95 = 5700; Males: 50 × 90 = 4500. Then add these two amounts together and divide by the total number of students in the class to get your solution: (5700 + 4500) ÷ 110 = 10,200 ÷ 110 = 92.73 average for all 110 students

229) The correct answer is D. The question is asking us about a time duration of 6 minutes, so we need to calculate the amount of seconds in 6 minutes: 6 minutes × 60 seconds per minute = 360 seconds in total. Then divide the total time by the amount of time needed to make one journey: 360 seconds ÷ 45 seconds per journey = 8 journeys. Finally, multiply the number of journeys by the amount of inches per journey in order to get the total inches: 10.5 inches for 1 journey × 8 journeys = 84 inches in total

230) The correct answer is B. First of all, add up to find the total number of customers: 40 + 30 + 20 + 30 = 120 customers in total for all four regions. The salespeople received $540 in total, so we need to divide this by the amount of customers: $540 ÷ 120 customers = $4.50 per customer

231) The correct answer is D. The plumber is going to earn $4,000 for the month. He charges a set fee of $100 per job, and he will do 5 jobs, so we can calculate the total set fees first: $100 set fee per job × 5 jobs = $500 total set fees. Then deduct the set fees from the total for the month in order to determine the total for the hourly pay: $4,000 – $500 = $3,500. He earns $25 per hour, so divide the hourly rate into the total hourly pay in order to determine the number of hours he will work: $3,500 total hourly pay ÷ $25 per hour = 140 hours to work

232) The correct answer is B. 45% of the freshman, 30% of the sophomores, 38% of the juniors, and 30% of the seniors will attend. Since each of the four grade levels has roughly the same number of students, we can simply divide by 4 to get the average. Calculating the average, we get the overall percentage for all four grades: (45 + 30 + 38 + 30) ÷ 4 = 35.75%. 35% is the closest answer to 35.75%, so it best approximates our result.

233) The correct answer is C. Step 1 – Determine the commission earned per hour: $15 charged – $12 paid to employee = $3 per hour commission. Step 2 – Calculate the total hours that the 10 employees worked: 10 × 40 = 400 hours in total. Step 3 – Multiply the total number of hours by the commission per hour to solve: 400 hours × $3 commission per hour = $1,200 total commission

234) The correct answer is D. Divide to solve: 49 ÷ 50 = 0.98 = 98%

235) The correct answer is D. Step 1 – Add the whole numbers: 8 + 7 = 15. Step 2 – Add the fractions: 3/4 + 1/2 = 3/4 + 2/4 = 5/4. Step 3 – Simplify the fraction from Step 2: 5/4 = 4/4 + 1/4 = $1\frac{1}{4}$ = 1 foot and 3 inches. Step 4 – Combine the results from Step 1 and Step 3 to solve the problem: 15 feet + 1 foot and 3 inches = 16 feet and 3 inches

236) The correct answer is C. In this problem, the fraction on the second number is larger than the fraction on the first number, so we need to covert the first fraction before we start our calculation. Step 1 – Convert $28\frac{3}{10}$ for subtraction: $28\frac{3}{10} = 27\frac{3}{10} + 1 = 27\frac{3}{10} + \frac{10}{10} = 27\frac{13}{10}$. Step 2 – Subtract the whole numbers. $7\frac{9}{10}$ hours have been spent on the job so far, so subtract the 7 hours: 27 – 7 = 20. Step 3 – Subtract the fractions: 13/10 – 9/10 = 4/10. Step 4 – Simplify the fraction from Step 3: 4/10 = (4 ÷ 2)/(10 ÷ 2) = 2/5. Step 4 – Combine the results from Step 2 and Step 4 to get your new mixed number to solve the problem: 20 + 2/5 = $20\frac{2}{5}$

237) The correct answer is C. Step 1 – Take the 147 parts of blue slate chippings for this order and divide by the 3 parts stated in the original ratio: 147 ÷ 3 = 49. Step 2 – Multiply the result from Step 1 by the 2 parts of white gravel stated in the original ratio to get your answer: 49 × 2 = 98

238) The correct answer is B. We need to set up a fraction, the numerator of which consists of the amount of sales in dollars for sweatpants, and the denominator of which consists of the total amount of sales in dollars for both items. The problem tells us that the amount of sales in dollars for sweatpants is 30s and the total amount of sales is 850, so the answer is 30s/850.

239) The correct answer is D. Step 1 – Determine the excess amount over the amount for the deal: 100 bottles needed – (4 cases × 24 bottles each) = 100 – 96 = 4 individual bottles left. Step 2 – Take the result from the previous step and multiply by the individual price: 4 × $2.50 = $10. Step 3 – Determine the cost of the 4 cases: 4 × $50 = $200. Step 4 – Add the results from the previous two steps to get the total wholesale price for the deal: $200 + $10 = $210

240) The correct answer is A. Step 1 – Covert the grams to ounces: 1190.7 ÷ 28.35 = 42. Step 2 – Add the result from step 1 to the amount of ounces for the US order to solve: 39 + 42 = 81 ounces

241) The correct answer is B. Step 1 – Find the area of the ceiling. The formula for the area of a rectangle is (length × width). So, substitute the values to find the area: (35 × 25) = 875 square feet. Step 2 – Find the area of each ceiling tile. The measurements for our tiles are given in inches: 6 inches by 6 inches = 36

square inches. Step 3 – Calculate how many square inches there are in a square foot: 12 inches by 12 inches = 144 square inches. Step 4 – Determine how many tiles you need per square foot: 144 square inches ÷ 36 square inches per tile = 4 tiles per square foot. Step 5 – Multiply to solve: 875 square feet in total × 4 tiles per square foot = 3,500 tiles needed

242) The correct answer is B. From the formula sheet, we can see that 1 milligram = 0.001 gram. We are converting milligrams to grams, so we are doing the formula in the correct order, rather than in reverse. Therefore, multiply by 0.001 to solve: 1,275,000 milligrams × 0.001 = 1,275 grams

243) The correct answer is B. Step 1 – Find the radius: The diameter is 10 inches, so the radius is 5 inches. Step 2 – Cube the radius for the formula: 5 × 5 × 5 = 125. Then multiply by 3.14 and 4/3 to find the volume of the sphere: 125 × 3.14 × 4/3 = 523.33, which we round to 523.

244) The correct answer is B. To calculate a reverse percentage you need to divide, rather than multiply. So, take the $12 retail price and divide by 625%, which is 100% for the cost plus 525% for the markup: $12 ÷ 625% = $12 ÷ 6.25 = $1.92

245) The correct answer is D. The perimeter of rectangle is 2(*length* + *width*). So, determine the total width for both sides: 2 × 75 = 150. Now deduct this amount from the perimeter: 350 − 150 = 200. Finally, divide this result by 2 to get the length: 200 ÷ 2 = 100

246) The correct answer is A. Step 1 – Calculate the cubic feet for each box: length × width × height = 3 × 3 × 2 = 18 cubic feet per box. Step 2 – Determine how much of the product is on hand. The first box is $^1/_6$ full, the second box is $^1/_2$ full, and the third box is $^2/_3$ full: $^1/_6$ + $^1/_2$ + $^2/_3$ = $^1/_6$ + $^3/_6$ + $^4/_6$ = $^8/_6$.= 1$^2/_6$ = 1$^1/_3$ boxes left. Step 3 – Determine how much is required to replenish the stock: 3 boxes needed – 1$^1/_3$ boxes on hand = 1$^2/_3$ boxes needed. Step 4 – Determine how many cubic feet are needed: 1$^2/_3$ boxes × 18 cubic feet per box = 30 cubic feet needed. Step 5 – Calculate the cost: 30 cubic feet needed × $9 per cubic foot = $270

247) The correct answer is D. The range is the highest number minus the lowest number. Our data set is: $65000, $52000, $125000, $89000, $36000, $84000, $31000, $135000, $74000, and $87000. So, the range is: $135000 − $31000 = $104000

248) The correct answer is B. 205,346.9781 ÷ 1,000 = 205.3469781. The hundreds place is three places to the left of the decimal point, so 2 is in the hundreds place.

249) The correct answer is A. For algebraic equivalency questions like this, you can perform the operations on each of the answer choices to see which one is equivalent. Remember to be careful when performing multiplication on negative numbers inside parentheticals.
6 + 2(15 − *x*) =
6 + (2 × 15) + (2 × −*x*) =
6 + 30 − 2*x* =
36 − 2*x*

250) The correct answer is A. − 63 + 17 = − 46; the absolute value of this is 46, and the negative of the absolute value is − 46.

251) The correct answer is A. We know from the calculations in the answer to the previous question that the gray area is 18 square yards and the white area is 45 square yards. So, the ratio is 18:45. Both of these numbers are divisible by 9, so we can simplify the ratio to 2:5 (18 ÷ 9 = 2 and 45 ÷ 9 = 5)

252) The correct answer is D. When looking at scatterplots, try to see if the dots are roughly grouped into any kind of pattern or line. If so, positive or negative relationships may be represented. Here, however, the dots are located at what appear to be random places on all four quadrants of the graph. So, the scatterplot suggests that no relationship can be discerned.

253) The correct answer is A. We can see that cars account for the largest number of accidents on all of the four dates. So, cars will also account for the largest combined total for the four dates.

254) The correct answer is B. Substitute 8 for x to solve.
$x^2 - 5x - 9 =$
$8^2 - (5 \times 8) - 9 =$
$64 - 40 - 9 =$
15

255) The correct answer is A. Get rid of the integer on the left by adding 9 to each side of the equation.
$5x - 9 = 6$
$5x - 9 + 9 = 6 + 9$
$5x = 15$
Then divide each side by 5 to isolate x and solve.
$5x \div 5 = 15 \div 5$
$x = 3$

256) The correct answer is D. Divide each side of the equation by 3. Then subtract 5 from both sides of the equation as shown below.
$18 = 3(x + 5)$
$18 \div 3 = [3(x + 5)] \div 3$
$6 = x + 5$
$6 - 5 = x + 5 - 5$
$1 = x$

257) The correct answer is D. Place the integers on one side of the inequality.
$-3x + 14 < 5$
$-3x + 14 - 14 < 5 - 14$
$-3x < -9$
Then get rid of the negative number. We need to reverse the way that the inequality sign points because we are dividing by a negative.
$-3x < -9$
$-3x \div -3 > -9 \div -3$ ("Less than" becomes "greater than" because we divide by a negative number.)
$x > 3$
3.15 is greater than 3, so it is the correct answer.

258) The correct answer is D. Isolate the whole numbers to one side of the equation first.

$$20 - \frac{3x}{4} \geq 17$$

$$(20 - 20) - \frac{3x}{4} \geq 17 - 20$$

$$- \frac{3x}{4} \geq -3$$

Then get rid of the fraction.

$$- \frac{3x}{4} \geq -3$$

$$\left(4 \times -\frac{3x}{4}\right) \geq -3 \times 4$$

$$-3x \geq -12$$

Then deal with the remaining whole numbers.

$$-3x \geq -12$$

$$-3x \div -3 \geq -12 \div -3$$

$$x \leq 4$$

Remember to reverse the way the sign points when you divide by a negative number.

259) The correct answer is B. The mean is the arithmetic average. First, add up all of the items: –2% + 5% + 7.5% + 14% + 17% + 1.3% + –3% = 39.8%. Then divide by 7 since there are 7 companies in the set: 39.8% ÷ 7 = 5.68% ≈ 5.7%

260) The correct answer is C. The problem states that the salesperson gets a $12 commission for every order greater than $100, so we need to multiply the amount of the commission by the number of orders over $100 first of all: $12 × 32 = $384. Then add this to the basic pay to get the total for the month: $1250 + $384 = $1634

261) The correct answer is B. Divide the total amount of sales by the price per unit to solve: $310 ÷ $12.40 = 25 units sold

262) The correct answer is D. The ratio of bags of apples to bags of oranges is 2 to 3, so for every two bags of apples, there are three bags of oranges. First, take the total amount of bags of apples and divide by the 2 from the original ratio: 44 ÷ 2 = 22. Then multiply this by 3 to determine how many bags of oranges are in the store: 22 × 3 = 66

263) The correct answer is B. At the beginning of January, there are 300 students, but 5% of the students leave during the month, so we have 95% left at the end of the month: 300 × 95% = 285. Then 15 students join on the last day of the month, so we add that back in to get the total at the end of January: 285 + 15 = 300. If this pattern continues, there will always be 300 students in the academy at the end of any month.

264) The correct answer is D. Calculate the discount: $120 × 12.5% = $15 discount. Then subtract the discount from the original price to determine the sales price: $120 – $15 = $105

265) The correct answer is A. The ratio of defective chips to functioning chips is 1 to 20. So, the defective chips form one group and the functioning chips form another group. Therefore, the total data set can be divided into groups of 21. Accordingly, $1/21$ of the chips will be defective. The factory produced 11,235 chips last week, so we calculate as follows: 11,235 × $1/21$ = 535

266) The correct answer is C. The fine for speeding is $50 per violation, so the total amount collected for speeding violations was: 60 speeding violations × $50 per violation = $3000. There 90 other violations, and the fine for other violations is $20, so the total for other violations is: 90 × $20 = $1800. Next, we need to deduct these two amounts from the total collections of $6,000 in order to find out how much was collected for parking violations: $6000 – $3000 – $1800 = $1200 in total for parking violations. There were 30 parking violations. We divide to get the answer: $1200 income for parking violations ÷ 30 parking violations = $40 each

267) The correct answer is B. The original price of the sofa on Wednesday was x. On Thursday, the sofa was reduced by 10%, so the price on Thursday was 90% of x or $0.90x$. On Friday, the sofa was reduced by a further 15%, so the price on Friday was 85% of the price on Thursday, so we can multiply Thursday's price by 0.85 to get our answer: $(0.90)(0.85)x$

268) The correct answer is B. Assign a variable for the age of each boy. Alex = A, Burt = B, and Zander = Z. Alex is twice as old as Burt, so A = 2B. Burt is one year older than three times the age of Zander, so B = 3Z + 1. Then substitute the value of B into the first equation.

A = 2B

A = 2(3Z + 1)

A = 6Z + 2

So, Alex is 2 years older than 6 times the age of Zander.

269) The correct answer is A. Step 1 – Add the whole numbers: 37 + 25 = 62. Step 2 – Add the fractions: 2/5 + 4/5 = 6/5 = $1^1/_5$. Step 3 – Combine the results from Step 1 and Step 2 to get your new mixed number to solve the problem: 62 + $1^1/_5$ = $63^1/_5$

270) The correct answer is C. Step 1 – Take the total amount of customers expected and divide by the 3 stated in the original ratio: 15 ÷ 3 = 5. Step 2 – Take the amount from Step 1 and multiply by 1 from the original ratio to solve the problem: 5 × 1 = 5

271) The correct answer is D. Step 1 – Calculate the amount of time spent on the initial job: 9:15 AM to 10:25 AM = 1 hour and 10 minutes = 70 minutes. Step 2 – Calculate the rate per square yard: 70 minutes ÷ 7 square yards = 10 minutes per square yard. Step 3 – Multiply the figure from Step 2 by the total amount of square yards to paint: 17.5 square yards × 10 minutes per square yard = 175 minutes = 2 hours and 55 minutes. Step 4 – Determine the time of completion: 9:15 AM + 2 hours and 55 minutes = 11:15 AM + 55 minutes = 12:10 PM

272) The correct answer is A. Add the three figures together to solve: 1235.35 + 567.55 + 347.25 = 2150.15 units

273) The correct answer is D. Step 1 – Add the whole numbers: 19 + 14 = 33. Step 2 – Add the fractions: 3/4 + 3/4 = 6/4. Step 3 – Simplify the fraction from Step 2: 6/4 = $1^2/_4$ = $1^1/_2$. Step 4 – Combine the results from Step 1 and Step 3 to solve the problem: 33 + $1^1/_2$ = $34^1/_2$

274) The correct answer is A. In this problem, the fraction on the second number is larger than the fraction on the first number, so we need to covert the first fraction before we start our calculation. Step 1 – Convert the first mixed number for subtraction: $102^7/_{18}$ = $101^7/_{18}$ + 1 = $101^7/_{18}$ + $^{18}/_{18}$ = $101^{25}/_{18}$. Step 2 – Subtract the whole numbers: 101 – 24 = 77. Step 3 – Subtract the fractions: 25/18 – 11/18 = 14/18. Step 4 – Simplify the fraction from Step 3: 14/18 = (14 ÷ 2)/(18 ÷ 2) = 7/9. Step 5 – Combine the results from Step 2 and Step 4 to get your new mixed number to solve the problem: 77 + 7/9 = $77^7/_9$.

275) The correct answer is B. In order to make the estimate, round each item up or down to the nearest pound. The weights in the problem were 5.14, 4.98, 3.20, 8.78. We round these to 5, 5, 3, and 9. Then add these together and add 1 more pound for the box: 5 + 5 + 3 + 9 + 1 = 23

276) The correct answer is D. Circumference ≈ diameter × 3.14. The circumference of the first circle is calculated as follows: diameter × 3.14 = 10 × 3.14 = 31.4. The circumference of the second circle is as follows: diameter × 3.14 = 6 × 3.14 = 18.84. The difference in the circumferences is: 31.4 – 18.84 = 12.56

277) The correct answer is C. Perimeter = 2L + 2W = (2 × 18) + (2 × 10) = 36 + 20 = 56

105

278) The correct answer is D. The circumference of a circle is approximately 3.14 times the diameter. The partition is going to divide the circular arena in half, so the partition will be placed on the diameter of the circle. So divide to calculate the diameter in feet: 1,017.36 ÷ 3.14 = 324 feet

279) The correct answer is D. Step 1 – Determine the percentage of the discount on Product A: $4 discount ÷ $20 original price = 20% discount. Step 2 – Calculate the dollar value of the discount on Product B: $16 × 20% = $3.20. Step 3 – Subtract the dollar value of the discount on Product B from the normal price to get the discounted price of Product B: $16 - $3.20 = $12.80

280) The correct answer is C. We need to calculate the volume in cubic inches: 10 inches × 7 inches × 5 inches = 350 cubic inches

281) The correct answer is D. Step 1 – Take the 14 cups for this batch and divide by the 2 cups stated in the original ratio: 14 ÷ 2 = 7. Step 2 – Multiply the result from Step 1 by the 3 ounces of herbal therapy product stated in the original ratio to get your answer: 3 × 7 = 21

282) The correct answer is B. We don't know the age of the 10th car, so put this in as x to solve:
(2 + 3 + 4 + 5 + 6 + 7 + 9 + 10 + 12 + x) ÷ 10 = 6
[(2 + 3 + 4 + 5 + 6 + 7 + 9 + 10 + 12 + x) ÷ 10] × 10 = 6 × 10
2 + 3 + 4 + 5 + 6 + 7 + 9 + 10 + 12 + x = 60
58 + x = 60
x = 2

283) The correct answer is C. Three out of ten students are taking the class. So, here we have the proportion 3 to 10. Step 1 – Divide the total number of students by the second number in the proportion to get the number of groups: 650 ÷ 10 = 65 groups. Step 2 – Multiply the number of groups by the first number in the proportion in order to get the result: 3 × 65 = 195 art students.

284) The correct answer is C. 4 quarts of cranberry juice at $3 per quart cost $12 since 3 × $4 = $12. He paid $18 for the entire purchase, so subtract to get the total amount spent on orange juice: $18 – $12 = $6. Orange juice costs $2 per quart, so divide to determine how much orange juice he bought: $6 ÷ $2 each = 3 quarts of orange juice.

285) The correct answer is B. Our facts were: 5 more than 4 times the number x is equal to the number y. Build up your equation based on each part of the problem.
4 times the number x: 4x
5 more than 4 times the number x: 4x + 5
5 more than 4 times the number x is equal to the number y: : 4x + 5 = y

286) The correct answer is B. The original recipe was for 4 brownies but we are making 6 brownies, so we can set up the following fraction to get our proportion: 6/4 = 4/4 + 2/4 = 1 + ½ = 1½. For 6 brownies, we need to use 1½ of all of the ingredients listed on the original recipe, and the original recipe calls for ½ teaspoon of vanilla extract: ½ teaspoon × 1½ = [(½ × 1) + (½ × ½)] = ½ + ¼ = ¾

287) The correct answer is C. When you see numbers inside two lines like this, you are being asked for the absolute value. Absolute value is always a positive number. For example, | −7| = 7. So, first of all we need to perform the operation inside the absolute value signs. |5 − 8| = | −3| = 3. However, here we have

a negative sign in front of the absolute value. Therefore, we need to make the result negative since there is a negative sign in front of the absolute value: $-|5-8| = -|-3| = -|3| = -3$

288) The correct answer is D. Get the integers to one side of the equation first of all.

$$\frac{1}{5}x + 3 = 5$$

$$\frac{1}{5}x + 3 - 3 = 5 - 3$$

$$\frac{1}{5}x = 2$$

Then multiply to eliminate the fraction and solve the problem.

$$\frac{1}{5}x \times 5 = 2 \times 5$$

$$x = 10$$

289) The correct answer is C. The quantity of diseases is indicated on the bottom of the graph, while the number of children is indicated on the left side of the graph. To determine the amount of children that have been vaccinated against three or more diseases, we need to add the amounts represented by the bars for 3, 4, and 5 diseases: 30 + 20 + 10 = 60 children

290) The correct answer is B. The question is asking us to calculate one third of one half. So, we multiply to get our answer: $\frac{1}{2} \times \frac{1}{3} = \frac{(1 \times 1)}{(2 \times 3)} = \frac{1}{6}$

291) The correct answer is C. Essentially a rectangle is missing at the upper left-hand corner of the figure. We would need to know both the length and width of the "missing" rectangle in order to calculate the area of our figure. So, we need to know both X and Y in order to solve the problem.

292) The correct answer is D. An equilateral triangle has three equal sides and three equal angles. Since all 3 angles in any triangle need to add up to 180 degrees, each angle of an equilateral triangle is 60 degrees (180 ÷ 3 = 60). Angles that lie along the same side of a straight line must add up to 180. So, we calculate angle a as follows: 180 − 60 = 120

293) The correct answer is B. The two sides of the field form a right angle, so we can use the Pythagorean Theorem to solve the problem: $\sqrt{3^2 + 4^2} = \sqrt{9 + 16} = \sqrt{25} = 5$

294) The correct answer is B. We know that any straight line is 180°. We also know that the sum of the degrees of the three angles of any triangle is 180°. The sum of angles X, Y, and Z = 180. So, the sum of angle X and angle Z equals 180° − 30° = 150°. Remember that in an isosceles triangle, the angles at the base of the triangle are equal. Because this triangle is isosceles, angle X and angle Z are equivalent. So, we can divide the remaining degrees by 2 as follows: 150° ÷ 2 = 75° In other words, angle X and angle Z are each 75°. Then we need to subtract the degree of the angle $\angle$X from 180° to get the measurement of $\angle$WXY. 180° − 75° = 105°

295) The correct answer is C. Divide and then express the result as a percentage. Step 1 – Treat the line in the fraction as the division symbol: $9/16 = 9 \div 16 = 0.5625$. Step 2 – To express the result from Step 1 as a percentage, move the decimal point two places to the right and add the percent sign: $0.5625 = 56.25\%$

296) The correct answer is A. Since this is a bell-shaped curve, two possible amounts of sleep are possible for certain quantities of sugar consumption .

297) The correct answer is C. Our number is: 473.862. The tenths place is the first number to the right of the decimal, which is 8 in our number. This is followed by a 6, so we have to round up to 9.

298) The correct answer is B. Subtract the decimal from 1 to find the decimal amount left: $1 - 0.05 = 0.95$. Then multiply the total number of employees at the start of the year by this decimal number:
$120 \times 0.95 = 114$ employees left

299) The correct answer is D. 20 percent is equal to 0.20. We are doing a reverse percentage, so we need to divide to solve: $\$60 \div 0.20 = \$300$. We can check this result as follows: $300 \times 0.20 = 60$

300) The correct answer is A. First, subtract whole numbers: $6 - 2 = 4$. Then subtract fractions: $^3/_4 - ^1/_2 = ^3/_4 - ^2/_4 = ^1/_4$. Put them together for the result: $4^1/_4$

301) The correct answer is B. Set up the proportion as a fraction: 9 ounces of liquid for every 6 of ounces active chemical $= ^9/_6$. Then simplify the fraction: $^9/_6 \div ^3/_3 = ^3/_2$. Now, multiply the fraction by the amount for the current job to solve: $^3/_2 \times 10 = ^{30}/_2 = 30 \div 2 = 15$

302) The correct answer is B. First you need to find the total points. You do this by taking the erroneous average times 5: $5 \times 96 = 480$. Then you need to divide the total points earned by the correct number of surveys to get the correct average: $480 \div 6 = 80$

303) The correct answer is C. You have 3 partial trays of unsold brownies at the end of the day, and each tray has $^1/_8$ of the brownies left in it, so in total you have $^3/_8$ of a tray left. You need to divide this by 4 employees. When you are asked to divide fractions, remember that you need to invert the second fraction. Here we have the whole number 4. 4 inverted is $^1/_4$. So, multiply the fractions to solve: $^3/_8 \times ^1/_4 = {^{(3 \times 1)}}/_{(8 \times 4)} = ^3/_{32}$

304) The correct answer is A. Represent the mixed numbers as decimal numbers: Person 1: $14^3/_4 = 14.75$; Person 2: $20^1/_5 = 20.20$; Person 3: 36.35. Then add all three amounts together to find the total: $14.75 + 20.20 + 36.35 = 71.30$

305) The correct answer is C. The office purchased 50 reams of paper this month and has used 5 of them, so you need to divide to solve $5 \div 50 = 0.10$

306) The correct answer is D. First of all, you have to calculate the total amount of points earned by the entire group. Multiply the female average by the amount of female candidates. Total points for females: $87 \times 55 = 4785$. Then multiply the male average by the amount of males. Total points for male

candidates: 80 × 45 = 3600. Then add these two amounts together to find out the total points scored by the entire group. Total points for entire group: 4785 + 3600 = 8385. When you have calculated the total amount of points for the entire group, you divide this by the total number of candidates to get the average: 8385 ÷ 100 = 83.85

307) The correct answer is A. We know that Mary has already gotten 80% of the money. However, the question is asking how much money she still needs: 100% – 80% = 20% = 0.20. Now do the multiplication: 650 × 0.20 = 130

308) The correct answer is B. They buy 4 of product A at $5 each, so they buy $20 worth of product A. They paid $60 in total, so subtract the total cost of product A from the overall total to calculate the total spent on Product B: $60 – $20 = $40. Product B costs $8 each, so divide to solve: $40 spent on Product B ÷ $8 each = 5 units

309) The correct answer is C. She bought 3 pairs of shoes, so determine the amount spent on shoes: 3 pairs of shoes × $25 each= $75. Then deduct this from the total amount of the purchase to calculate how much she spent on socks: $85 – $75 = $10. The socks cost $2 a pair, so divide to solve: $10 ÷ $2 each = 5 pairs

310) The correct answer is C. Step 1 – Determine the price per yard: $10.50 per 1/2 yard × 2 = $21.00 per yard. Step 2 – Calculate the price for 20 yards: 20 × $21.00 = $420.00. Step 3 – The customer purchased 20 and a half yards, so the price of the remaining half yard is $10.50. Add this to the result from Step 2 to get your answer: $420.00 + $10.50 = $430.50

311) The correct answer is D. Step 1 – Add the whole numbers: 49 + 18 = 67. Step 2 – Add the fractions: 3/16 + 1/16 = 4/16 = 1/4. Step 3 – Combine the results from Step 1 and Step 2 to get your new mixed number to solve the problem: 67 + 1/4 = $67^1/_4$

312) The correct answer is B. Take the amount of defective SIM cards and divide by the total amount of SIM cards: 11 ÷ 132 = 0.083 = 8.3%, which we round to 8%.

313) The correct answer is A. Step 1 – Take the total amount of flour required for this batch and divide by the 9 stated in the original ratio: 126 ÷ 9 = 14. Step 2 – Take the amount from Step 1 and multiply by 2 from the original ratio to solve the problem: 14 × 2 = 28

314) The correct answer is B. Step 1 – Calculate the amount of time spent on the initial job: 12:10 to 2:25 = 2 hours and 15 minutes = 135 minutes. Step 2 – Calculate the rate per cap: 135 minutes ÷ 3 caps = 45 minutes per cap. Step 3 – Calculate how many minutes there are in 9 hours: 9 hours × 60 minutes = 540 minutes. Step 4 – Divide to solve: 540 minutes available ÷ 45 minutes per cap = 12 caps

315) The correct answer is D. An inverse relationship exists when one thing goes down as the other thing goes up. The graph shows that students have fewer incorrect answers when they spend more hours studying. So, there is an inverse relationship between the amount of incorrect answers and the number of hours a student spends studying.

316) The correct answer is C. The circumference of a circle is calculated by using this formula: Circumference ≈ 3.14 × diameter. The diameter of a circle is always equal to the radius times 2. So, the diameter for this circle is 4 × 2 = 8. Therefore, the approximate circumference is: 8 × 3.14 = 25.12

317) The correct answer is D. Area of a circle $\approx 3.14 \times \text{radius}^2$. The radius of this circle is 6, and $6^2 = 36$. Therefore, the area is approximately: $36 \times 3.14 = 113.04$

318) The correct answer is B. The area of circle A is $0.4^2 \times 3.14 = 0.16 \times 3.14 = 0.5024$. The area of circle B is $0.2^2 \times 3.14 = 0.04 \times 3.14 = 0.1256$. Then subtract: $0.5024 - 0.1256 = 0.3768$

319) The correct answer is D. The volume of a box is calculated by taking the length times the width times the height: $5 \times 6 \times 10 = 300$

320) The correct answer is B. Triangle area = (base × height) ÷ 2. Substitute the amounts for base and height: area = $(5 \times 2) \div 2 = 10 \div 2 = 5$

321) The correct answer is B. Cone volume = $(3.14 \times \text{radius}^2 \times \text{height}) \div 3$. Substitute the values for base and height. volume = $(3.14 \times 3^2 \times 4) \div 3 = (3.14 \times 9 \times 4) \div 3 = 3.14 \times 36 \div 3 = 37.68$

322) The correct answer is B. Remember that the perimeter is the measurement along the outside edges of the rectangle or other area. The formula for perimeter is as follows: $P = 2W + 2L$. If the room is 12 feet by 10 feet, we need 12 feet × 2 to finish the long sides of the room and 10 feet × 2 to finish the shorter sides of the room. $(2 \times 10) + (2 \times 12) = 20 + 24 = 44$. Each piece of wood is one foot long, so 44 pieces are needed to finish the room.

323) The correct answer is A. The area of a circle is $3.14 \times \text{radius}^2$. Radius is half of diameter, and in our problem the diameter is 36, so the radius is 18. So, put the values into the formula to solve: $3.14 \times 18 \times 18 = 1,017$

324) The correct answer is D. To find the mean, add up all of the items in the set and then divide by the number of items in the set. Here we have 7 numbers in the set, so we get our answer as follows: $(89 + 65 + 75 + 68 + 82 + 74 + 86) \div 7 = 539 \div 7 = 77$

325) The correct answer is B. Our data set is: 2.5, 9.4, 3.1, 1.7, 3.2, 8.2, 4.5, 6.4, 7.8. First, put the numbers in ascending order: 1.7, 2.5, 3.1, 3.2, 4.5, 6.4, 7.8, 8.2, 9.4. The median is the number in the middle of the set: 1.7, 2.5, 3.1, 3.2, **4.5**, 6.4, 7.8, 8.2, 9.4

326) The correct answer is C. Substitute –2 for x to solve.
$2x^2 - x + 5 =$
$[2 \times (-2^2)] - (-2) + 5 =$
$[2 \times (4)] - (-2) + 5 =$
$(2 \times 4) + 2 + 5 =$
$8 + 2 + 5 = 15$

327) The correct answer is A. Isolate x to solve. You do this by doing the same operation on each side of the equation First, subtract 5 from each side to get rid of the integer 5 on the left side.
$-6x + 5 = -19$
$-6x + 5 - 5 = -19 - 5$

Then simplify.
$-6x + 5 - 5 = -19 - 5$
$-6x = -24$

Then divide each side by –6 to isolate *x*.

–6*x* = –24

–6*x* ÷ –6 = –24 ÷ –6

x = –24 ÷ –6

x = 4

328) The correct answer is A. Perform the multiplication on the terms in the parentheses.

2(3*x* – 1) = 4(*x* + 1) – 3

6*x* – 2 = (4*x* + 4) – 3

Then simplify.

6*x* – 2 = (4*x* + 4) – 3

6*x* – 2 = 4*x* + 1

6*x* – 2 – 1 = 4*x* + 1 – 1

6*x* – 3 = 4*x*

Then isolate *x* to get your answer.

6*x* – 3 = 4*x*

6*x* – 4*x* – 3 = 4*x* – 4*x*

2*x* – 3 = 0

2*x* – 3 + 3 = 0 + 3

2*x* = 3

2*x* ÷ 2 = 3 ÷ 2

$x = {}^3\!/_2$

329) The correct answer is D. Add the amounts for the first three bars together: 1.5 + 1.2 + 0.8 = 3.5

330) The correct answer is B. Our inequality is as follows: 125 – | – 94 + 107 | ≤ x. First work out the absolute value: |– 94 + 107 | = 13 and 125 – 13 = 112. So, a value of 112 for x will make the right side of the inequality equal to the left side. A value of 113 or higher will make the right side of the inequality greater than the left side. So x ≥ 112

ANSWER KEY

1) C

2) D

3) D

4) C

5) B

6) A

7) B

8) C

9) D

10) D

11) A

12) C

13) B

14) C

15) A

16) D

17) A

18) C

19) B

20) B

21) D

22) D

23) D

24) C

25) C

26) A

27) A

28) B

29) C

30) D

31) B

32) A

33) D

34) D

35) C

36) D

37) D

38) C

39) D

40) C

41) B

42) C

43) C

44) B

45) B

46) C

47) B

48) A

49) B

50) B

51) B

52) D

53) A

54) B

55) B

56) D

57) B

58) C

59) C

60) D

61) A

62) C

63) D

64) B

65) B

66) D

67) A

68) A

69) B

70) C

71) C

72) B

73) A

74) A

75) D

76) B

77) C

78) B

79) D

80) D

81) D

82) D

83) B

84) C

85) A

86) A

87) B

88) C

89) C

90) B

91) B

92) C

93) C

94) C

95) D

96) A

97) B

98) C

99) D

100) A

101) D

102) A

103) C

104) B

105) A

106) D

107) B

108) A

109) D

110) D

111) D

112) A

113) A

114) D

115) C

116) B

117) A

118) D

119) A

120) A

121) B

122) D

123) D

124) C

125) C

126) D

127) B

128) C

129) A

130) B

131) A

132) B

133) B

134) A

135) D

136) C

137) A

138) B

139) D

140) D

141) C

142) D

143) B

144) B

145) D

146) D

147) D

148) C

149) C

150) D

151) C

152) D

153) D

154) A

155) B

156) C

157) C

158) C

159) B

160) C

161) A

162) B

163) B

164) B

165) B

166) C

167) C

168) D

169) D

170) D

171) C

172) C

173) A

174) B

175) B

176) D

177) D

178) B

179) C

180) A

181) A

182) B

183) C

184) D

185) C

186) A

187) B

188) D

189) C

190) C

191) D

192) C

193) A

194) B

195) A

196) B

197) B

198) C

199) A

200) C

201) B

202) C

203) B

204) C

205) D

206) D

207) C

208) A

209) B

210) C

211) B

212) A

213) D

214) C

215) C

216) A

217) A

218) A

219) B

220) C

221) B

222) D

223) D

224) C

225) C

226) D

227) A

228) D

229) D

230) B

231) D

232) B

233) C

234) D

235) D

236) C

237) C

238) B

239) D

240) A

241) B

242) B

243) B

244) B

245) D

246) A

247) D

248) B

249) A

250) A

251) A

252) D

253) A

254) B

255) A

256) D

257) D

258) D

259) B

260) C

261) B

262) D

263) B

264) D

265) A

266) C

267) B

268) B

269) A

270) C

271) D

272) A

273) D

274) A

275) B

276) D

277) C

278) D

279) D

280) C

281) D

282) B

283) C

284) C

285) B

286) B

287) C

288) D

289) C

290) B

291) C

292) D

293) B

294) B

295) C

296) A

297) C

298) B

299) D

300) A

301) B

302) B

303) C

304) A

305) C

306) D

307) A

308) B

309) C

310) C

311) D

312) B

313) A

314) B

315) D

316) C

317) D

318) B

319) D

320) B

321) B

322) B

323) A

324) D

325) B

326) C

327) A

328) A

329) D

330) B

MATHEMATICS FORMULA SHEET

Weight
1 ounce ≈ 28.350 grams
1 pound = 16 ounces
1 pound ≈ 453.592 grams
1 milligram = 0.001 grams
1 kilogram = 1,000 grams
1 kilogram ≈ 2.2 pounds

Volume
1 cup = 8 fluid ounces
1 quart = 4 cups
1 gallon = 4 quarts
1 gallon = 231 cubic inches
1 liter ≈ 0.264 gallons
1 cubic foot = 1,728 cubic inches
1 cubic yard = 27 cubic feet

Distance
1 foot = 12 inches
1 yard = 3 feet
1 mile = 5,280 feet
1 mile ≈ 1.61 kilometers
1 inch = 2.54 centimeters
1 foot = 0.3048 meters
1 meter = 1,000 millimeters
1 meter = 100 centimeters
1 kilometer = 1,000 meters
1 kilometer ≈ 0.62 miles

Area
1 square foot = 144 square inches
1 square yard = 9 square feet

Circle
number of degrees in circle = 360°
circumference ≈ 3.14 × *diameter*
area ≈ 3.14 × (*radius*)^2

Triangle
sum of angles = 180°
area = ½ (*base* × *height*)

Rectangle
perimeter = 2(*length* + *width*)
area = *length* × *width*

Rectangular Solid (Box)
volume = *length* × *width* × *height*

Cube
volume = (*length of side*)^3

Cylinder
volume ≈ 3.14 × (*radius*)^2 × *height*

Cone
volume ≈ (3.14 × *radius*^{2} × *height*) ÷ 3

Sphere (Ball)
volume ≈ 4/3 × 3.14 × *radius*^{3}

Temperature
°C = 0.56(°F − 32) or 5/9(°F − 32)
°F = 1.8(°C) + 32 or (9/5 × °C) + 32

Made in the USA
San Bernardino, CA
02 June 2019